AFGHANISTAN

AUSTRIA

BAHRAIN

BERMUDA

CHINA

CUBA

EGYPT

ETHIOPIA

REPUBLIC OF GEORGIA

GERMANY

KUWAIT

IRAN

IRAQ

ISRAEL

MEXICO

NEW ZEALAND

PAKISTAN

RUSSIA

SAUDI ARABIA

SCOTLAND

SOUTH KOREA

UKRAINE

Afghanistan

Jeffrey A. Gritzner
University of Montana

Series Consulting Editor
Charles F. Gritzner
South Dakota State University

CHELSEA HOUSE
PUBLISHERS

A Haights Cross Communications 🗝️ Company

Frontispiece: Flag of Afghanistan adopted February 5, 2002.

Cover: Mosque at Mazar-e-Sharif, Afghanistan.

CHELSEA HOUSE PUBLISHERS

EDITOR IN CHIEF Sally Cheney
DIRECTOR OF PRODUCTION Kim Shinners
CREATIVE MANAGER Takeshi Takahashi
MANUFACTURING MANAGER Diann Grasse

Staff for AFGHANISTAN

EDITOR Lee Marcott
PRODUCTION ASSISTANT Jaimie Winkler
PICTURE RESEARCHER Pat Holl
COVER AND SERIES DESIGNER Takeshi Takahashi
LAYOUT 21st Century Publishing and Communications, Inc.

http://www.chelseahouse.com

5 7 9 8 6 4

Library of Congress Cataloging-in-Publication Data

Gritzner, Jeffrey A.
  Afghanistan / Jeffrey A. Gritzner.
    p. cm. — (Modern world nations)
Summary: A look at the geographic, political, economic, and social aspects of Afghanistan,
a country struggling to reconcile modernization with traditional values and ways.
Includes bibliographical references and index.
  ISBN 0-7910-6774-2 (hard) — ISBN 0-7910-7104-9 (pbk.)
  1. Afghanistan—Juvenile literature. [1. Afghanistan.] I. Title. II. Series.
DS351.5 .G75 2002
958.1—dc21

                                                                    2002007001

Table of Contents

Afghanistan

Afghan women in traditional dress are looking at woven carpets at a marketplace in Kabul.

Introducing
Afghanistan

Before the last two decades of warfare there, visitors to Afghanistan often had the feeling that they had stepped into the past. The cultural landscape was almost medieval in character. Massive vertical windmills in the Hari Rud Valley and the mosaics of carefully tended fields and gardens could both have been described by Arab geographers in the seventh century A.D. The traveler also would have seen many *karez* (or *qanat*)—enormous horizontal wells driven into the aquifers of distant mountains, whose presence is betrayed by the regularly spaced mounds of earth that snake across the landscape. These mounds mark the entrances of the vertical shafts that are used in the excavation and maintenance of the karez.

The visitor would have seen many picturesque walled villages with beehive-domed dwellings and bazaars enlivened by the sounds of artisans at work combined with the pungent odors of spices and herbs. One could visit an encampment of the *Pashtun* (*Pushtun* is the form most commonly used in Afghanistan) nomads, with their black goat's hair tents and often complaining camels. The name Pashtun is widely used to identify individuals or groups associated with the many Pashtun-speaking tribes of Afghanistan and Pakistan.

The Afghans themselves—proud, self-confident, and hospitable—are a people who have defied colonization and have defended their freedom in the face of the most powerful armies on Earth. In 1952, in his book *Beyond the High Himalaya,* Supreme Court Justice William O. Douglas wrote:

> We of the West have all the rudiments of civilization, all the dividends of a mounting standard of living. But the Afghans—one thousand years behind us in many respects—have a warmth of human relations that is often missing all the way from New York City to San Francisco.

Ironically, in recent decades both internal strife and the imposition of outside "civilization" upon the people of Afghanistan have contributed to the erosion of the "warmth of human relations" so admired by Justice Douglas and many others who know this land and its people.

The sturdiness of Afghanistan's people is matched by the country's natural landscapes. Rugged mountains and extensive desert plains dominate Afghanistan's physical geography. More than 100 peaks in the region's towering Pamir Knot—often called the "Roof of the World"—rise above 20,000 feet (6,100 meters), including many that are located in Afghanistan. The country's highest mountain, Nowshak, rises to 24,557 feet (7,485 meters), in Badakhshan Province—higher than any peak in the Western Hemisphere. Several peaks in the central ranges exceed 14,000 feet (4,270 meters) in elevation.

This vendor is selling his spices and food at his market stall in Jalalabad.

The region is geologically active and the mountains are still growing. This activity also contributes to frequent seismic (earthquake) activity that poses a constant threat to life and property. Despite their geologically young age, mountains have been deeply scoured by glaciers and running water. Precipitation is greatest in the highlands. Melting snowpack and mountain rains feed rivers, such as the Helmand. Its waters, as well as those of other streams, erode and deepen valleys, transport and deposit the sediment on the broad plains, and irrigate the semiarid lowlands.

One river scoured gorge, in particular, has become famous over several millennia. Khyber Pass, located on Afghanistan's eastern border with Pakistan, cuts through the Safed Koh range. Historically, it was one of the world's most important land routes linking the Mediterranean region and Southwest Asia with the subcontinent of India and present-day Pakistan. Southern Afghanistan's physical landscape is dominated by semiarid plains and parched deserts.

Mountain climates vary greatly. Upwind sides can be quite wet, whereas downwind sides can be extremely dry. Temperatures can be scorching on the desert floor at the foot of a mountain, while glaciers and permanent snow-fields cap the mountain's crest. In general, however, the country's summers are hot and dry and winters are cold, with heavy snowfall in the mountains. Average precipitation is roughly 13 inches (330 millimeters), with the extremes ranging from 36 inches (914 millimeters) in the Salang Pass area, to 2 inches (51 millmeters) in the southwestern deserts. Winds tend to blow from the north and northwest. During the summer, they are hot and often howling—accompanied by dust, and velocities that can reach 115 miles per hour (185 kilometers per hour). The summer winds of the southwestern deserts are known as the *bad-i-sad-u-bist ruz*—the "wind of 120 days."

The area now occupied by Afghanistan entered docu-mented history during the Bronze Age. The earliest Persian (Iranian) chronicles suggest that the region to the north and west of the Helmand River was dominated by nomadic, Indo-European-speaking Scythians. Eastern Afghanistan was dominated by Dravidian-speakers associ-ated with the Indus Civilization located to the east in present-day Pakistan. During the Aryan migrations of the second and first millennia B.C.E., Iranian tribes settled in the region and established several important kingdoms—including Bactria, the home of the prophet Zoroaster.

With the expansion of the Achaemenid Empire in the sixth century B.C.E., the kingdoms and principalities of Afghanistan comprised seven important *satrapies*, or provinces, of the empire: Gandhara (the Jalalabad area), Bactria, Merv, Herat, Sattagydia (the southeastern lowlands), Arachosia (Kandahar), and Zaranka (Sistan). The satrapies were, in a sense, the foundation of modern Afghanistan. The country has long been (and continues to be) sharply divided along provincial and ethnic lines.

The name *Afghanistan* simply means "Land of the Afghan." In the past, the term *Afghan* referred to Pashtun nomads. The term was then expanded to include all citizens of modern Afghanistan. There are many translations of the term Afghan. Some describe an arrogant or unruly people—terms applied by others in reference to the people who today bear the name. Some refer to a people courageous or free. Another interpretation refers to the spiritual station of the soul, characterized by one who has achieved purity. It is not known for certain when or why the name was first used.

Afghanistan is located in southern Central Asia. In some respects, it suffers from an inland location. Lack of direct access to the global sea has limited its contact with other places and peoples and has restricted trade with other lands. Its neighbors are Turkmenistan, Uzbekistan, and Tajikistan to the north (all former Soviet Republics); by the Xinjiang region of China through the Vakhan Corridor—a narrow strip of land extending eastward between Tajikistan and Pakistan; by Pakistan to the south and east; and by Iran to the west. With a total area of 252,092 square miles (653,089 square kilometers), Afghanistan is slightly smaller than Texas. It is also located roughly within the same latitudes as Texas, and both have resident populations of more than 20 million people.

In 2001, as a result of the tragic events associated with

High and rugged mountains dominate Afghanistan, the only landlocked country in the region. Lack of direct access to the global sea has limited its contact with other places and has restricted trade with other lands. It has an important strategic location between India and the Middle East.

terrorist attacks on the United States, Afghanistan has been catapulted onto the global stage. American writer Ambrose Bierce once said, "War is God's way of teaching Americans geography." Sadly, this seems to be true about interest in and knowledge of Afghanistan. As a result of the military action involving the United States and other countries in late 2001, people throughout the world have become much more aware of this quaint, traditional, isolated—yet important—country.

Jagged mountains provide the background for village life in the valleys.

2

The Natural Environment

F ew countries in the world have a more challenging natural landscape than Afghanistan. It is a world of towering mountains and broad desert plains. The rugged land has divided the country's regions and people—a chief factor contributing to Afghanistan's long history of regional and ethnic conflict. Ruggedness, combined with aridity, affects the economy as well. Not much of the land is suited to the raising of crops, a condition made even more troublesome by the country's low precipitation. Afghanistan also suffers from its landlocked condition, an interior location with no direct access to the sea. This chapter discusses the country's weather and climate, its landforms, its ecosystems, and its water features. Each element plays an important role in Afghanistan's historical and cultural geography.

Climate

There are three principal types of climate in Afghanistan: a midlatitude steppe and desert climate in the north; a variable highland climate in the eastern and central mountains; and a low-latitude tropical steppe and desert climate in the south. The relatively high elevation and continental character of Afghanistan result in significant annual and daily temperature changes. Kabul, at an elevation of 5,955 feet (1,815 meters), typically experiences a winter temperature range of 58° to -6°F (14° to −21°C), and a summer range of 101° to 58°F (38° to 11°C). A 50°F (10°C) temperature change from sunrise to early afternoon is possible.

Most precipitation arrives with the eastward penetration of moisture-laden air masses during the winter and spring. The average annual precipitation is 13 inches (330 millimeters). Summers and autumns are hot and dry. Predictably, humidity is low throughout most of the year. During summer and autumn afternoons, humidity often drops below 25 percent. Although levels of precipitation are lower in the south, the southern regions often receive some summer rains from the northward penetration of the Indian monsoon. During the summer and autumn, strong winds, the bad-i-sad-u-bist ruz, sweep out of the interior of Asia through a gap between the Paropamisus (Selseleh-ye) range in northwestern Afghanistan, and towering ranges to the west in neighboring Iran and Turkmenistan.

Land and Water Features

Afghanistan is a land of many contrasts. The natural landscape is composed of mountains, deeply cut valleys, and broad alluvial (land built from stream deposition) plains. The mountains are composed mainly of ancient sediments deposited under marine conditions. As segments of Gondwanaland moved (continental drift) northward during the Late Jurassic and Cretaceous periods (163 to 65 million years ago), these sediments were compressed and thrust upward, forming the great Alpine-Himalayan mountain belt. The belt remains geologically active, and earthquakes with magnitudes of 6.5 to 7.5 on the Richter scale are common. Nearly 10,000 people were killed by severe earthquakes in February 1998, and another 2,000 lost their lives in a devastating quake on the slopes of the Hindu Kush range in March 2002.

The Hindu Kush system extends westward from the Pamir Knot for some 700 miles (1,125 kilometers), almost reaching the Iranian border. Some simply regard the Safed Koh as a westerly extension of the Hindu Kush, rather than as a separate range. Among the other major ranges of the Hindu Kush complex are Koh-e Baba and the Torkestan Mountains. The mountains effectively divide Afghanistan into two regions, with the northern lowlands being smaller in area than those to the south. Within the highlands are many long, narrow basins—commonly the result of *grabens* (down-faulted blocks of earth). Extensive rolling plains are found near the Amu Darya in the north, the Helmand River in the south, around Kabul, and in Herat Province. The geological structures of Afghanistan are associated with a considerable variety and wealth of minerals. The rich store of mineral resources includes energy resources of natural gas, petroleum, and coal; the metals copper, iron ore, lead, and zinc; as well as talc, barites, sulfur, salt, and a considerable variety of precious and semiprecious stones.

Historically, Afghanistan's best known and perhaps most important landform feature has been the famous Khyber Pass. This narrow, steep-sided pass snakes for some 30 miles through the Safed Koh Mountains on the border between Afghanistan and Pakistan. Its highest point is about 3,500 feet (1,067 meters), well below the elevation of long and heavy winter snowfall. Although only about 12 feet (3 meters) wide in places, Khyber is one of the world's most famous mountain passes. It was a major link between the riches of India and Pakistan to the east, and Persia, Mesopotamia, and other wealthy and powerful lands to the west.

Both archaeology and history amply document the importance of the Khyber Pass over a period of at least 3,500 years. Conquering forces and caravans of traders found it to be the shortest and easiest land route between east and west. The Greek conqueror Alexander the Great may have been the first recorded user of the pass when, in 326 B.C.E., his army marched through the pass on its way to India. More than a thousand years later, Persian and Tartar troops stormed through the pass as they carried the Islamic faith into the Indus Valley and on to India. Mongols from the steppes of inner Asia also used the pass to invade and place their cultural imprint on Pakistan and India. More recently, the pass played an important role in 19th century Afghan wars fought by the British. Today a paved highway and traditional caravan route follow the pass, linking the cities of Kabul in Afghanistan and Peshawar in Pakistan.

Most of Afghanistan's important rivers rise in the central mountains. Because they are heavily dependent upon rainfall and melting snow, maximum flow is typically in the spring and early summer. During late summer, autumn, and winter, some rivers, such as the Khash Rud, are reduced to a series of unconnected pools in the streambed. There are four major river systems in Afghanistan: the Amu Darya in the north; the Helmand-Arghandab in the south; the Kabul in the east; and the Hari Rud in the west.

The Amu Darya flows along the Afghan borders with Tajikistan, Uzbekistan, and Turkmenistan for 680 miles (1,095 kilometers) before turning northwestward toward the Aral Sea. It is important for transportation, as well as for irrigation. Among its major tributaries are the Kowkcheh and Konduz. The waters of many tributaries are diverted for irrigation before reaching the Amu Darya.

The Helmand river system drains roughly 40 percent of Afghanistan. The river rises in the Koh-e Baba Range and flows

These fields in the Helmand Valley are irrigated by water from the Helmand River, which flows for about 800 miles.

for some 800 miles (1,290 kilometers), first in a southwesterly direction, and then northward, emptying into the Sistan Basin of Iran. As it flows southward, the Helmand is joined by the Arghandab near Lashkar Gah. The Arghandab rises to the north of Kandahar and, before joining the Helmand, loses much of its water to irrigated agriculture. The Kabul River is a tributary of the Indus River system. From its headwaters near Unai Pass west of Kabul, it flows some 225 miles (362 kilometers) in an easterly direction through the Kabul Valley, Daruntah Gorge, and the Jalalabad Plains before entering the Peshawar Valley and joining the Indus.

The Hari Rud flows almost due west from the Hesar Range in the central Hindu Kush. After passing through Herat and Eslam Qal'eh, the Hari Rud turns northward, forming roughly 100 miles (161 kilometers) of the Afghan-Iranian border before entering Turkmenistan. A second major river in western Afghanistan, the Morghab, similarly flows northward into Turkmenistan.

In an arid land, water is precious. Streams and groundwater are the source of both the domestic water supply and that used for irrigation—the lifeblood of Afghanistan's economy.

Many small streams and some lakes are intermittent; that is, they flow or contain water only after periods of precipitation, or spring snowmelt.

Soils and Ecosystems

Many things combine to create soils. The most important factors of soil formation are parent material (the rock material from which the soil is created), climate, plant and animal life, land forms, and the length of time over which these various elements have been at work. The soils of Afghanistan fall into two main categories. One is typical of dry climates; it is low in organic matter and is affected by the processes of calcification and salinization (accumulation of calcium and salt). The other category is alluvium, soils that are usually young or undeveloped; they are found in active slopes, basins, and flood plains. Factors of soil formation are important simply because these elements determine a soil's fertility.

Even though nearly two-thirds of the country's economy is based on agriculture, only about 12 percent of its land is suited to raising crops. Soil degradation (the process of making soils less fertile) can occur through erosion, the loss of vegetation cover as occurs in overgrazing and firewood cutting, and other processes. Afghanistan has experienced widespread loss of its soil resources. This is particularly true of the dry-climate soils as they are highly susceptible to the processes of salinization

Only about 12 percent of the land in Afghanistan is fertile enough for raising crops. Farmers must use springs and ground water for irrigation.

and waterlogging. Because soil formation takes a long time, the wise management and rebuilding of soil resources is an issue of considerable importance.

Afghanistan's natural vegetation has suffered from centuries of abuse. In the distant past, woodlands or dense grasses covered much of the country. Today, forests occupy a much smaller area than in the past, and many former

In Afghanistan the most heavily populated area is the northeast in the valley of the Kabul River. People also live in irrigated valleys around the fringes of the mountains that occupy a large part of the country. Many people also live on the foothills and steppes on the north side of the central mountains.

grassland regions are now semidesert or in some other degraded form. Elevation plays a key role in determining Afghanistan's ecosystems. With declining elevation, highland alpine tundra gives way to dense forests of needle leaf, coniferous, evergreen species; at still lower elevations, mixed woodlands and grasslands thrive; they, in turn, finally give way to semiarid steppe grasslands. Five major ecosystems dominate Afghanistan's landscapes.

Alpine tundra occurs at high elevations, above the tree line and below the level of permanent snow and ice. Its natural vegetation is composed of hardy grasses, small flowering plants, and stunted shrubs. The snow leopard, an occasional Siberian tiger, and brown bears are found in this harsh and remote natural environment.

Below the alpine tundra, warmer temperatures allow the growth of trees. This is the zone of montane forests, which occupy about 45 percent of the country. Vegetation includes pine, spruce, fir, and larch trees. Forests abound with animal life, including lynx and other large cats; wolves and foxes; ferrets, weasels, otters, martens, and badgers; as well as deer and wild sheep.

A semidesert ecosystem occurs in the cool northern lowland plains. Vegetation includes grasses and a variety of robust annual and perennial plants and shrubs. Wildlife includes a variety of birds; small animals such as hedgehogs, hares, and gophers; and larger carnivores such as wolves, jackals, and hyenas.

On the plains located south and west of the central highlands, midlatitude steppe (short grass) grasslands flourish. Broadleaf trees are often found along watercourses and in a few other locations favorable for their growth. Animal species include gazelles, wild pigs, jackals, and hyenas.

Finally, semidesert conditions prevail in the warm, semi-arid southern part of Afghanistan. Vegetation is composed mainly of short grasses, which are often scattered, rather than growing as a solid carpet. There are also a few woody perennials that are well adapted to the region's aridity. Wildlife is similar to that in the short-grass steppes, but also includes some fauna common to India, such as the mongoose, leopard, cheetah, and macaque (a monkey).

Wildlife

The highly mountainous country of Afghanistan contains a variety of ecological habitats. Although recent events have severely reduced wildlife populations in Afghanistan, the complex ecology of the country continues to support a remarkable diversity of wildlife.

Among the large cats of Afghanistan are snow leopards, leopards, jungle cats, and lynx. Other carnivores include the wolf, jackal, fox, hyena, mongoose, marbled polecat, ferret, weasel, otter, marten, badger, and brown bear. Among the herbivores are gazelle, several varieties of wild sheep, deer, and wild pig. The Rhesus monkey is also found in Afghanistan. Other animals include several species of hedgehogs, shrews, the Cape hare, squirrels, gophers, and groundhogs. There are also Indian crested porcupine; several species of rats, gerbils, voles, and mice; and a variety of bat species.

There are believed to be approximately 390 species of birds in Afghanistan, and several bird species are hunted for sport and food. Important game birds include partridges, pheasants, and quail. Some 80 species of wild pigeons and doves are found in Afghanistan, and large numbers of waterfowl arrive during the course of their spring and autumn migrations. Among the waterfowl are several species of ducks, grebes, geese, pelicans, and swans. There are also many shorebirds such as snipes, plovers, herons, storks, and cranes. The Baluch people of the marshy Sistan region are specialists in hunting and fishing. From their reed or dugout watercraft, they also snare birds with the same nets that they use for fishing.

There are many birds of prey, including eagles, hawks, falcons, and vultures. Among the smaller and more common birds are larks, warblers, sparrows, flycatchers, and swallows. Crows, magpies, and jays are familiar species found in areas of human habitation. Afghanistan also has large land turtles and a variety of frogs and toads. There are a dozen or so species of lizards, including the monitor lizard, which grows to a length of six feet (almost two meters). Among the many snakes are several that are highly poisonous. They include two species of cobra, the brightly banded and deadly krait, and several vipers. Scorpions, some of which are poisonous, are also found throughout the dry lands of the country.

Fish abound in the watercourses of Afghanistan, but are not widely used as a food resource. This may be due to the considerable distance most people live from fresh water and the fact that fish meat is highly perishable. German brown trout are found in streams north of the Hindu Kush, and rainbow trout have been released in the Salang and Panjshir Rivers. Four varieties of carp were introduced from China in the late 1960s. This was done in the hope that fish would become a more important source of food for many of the country's poor, rural people. In the warmer waters of the Amu Darya, a form of European catfish, the *laka*, often grows to more than seven feet (two meters) in length. Freshwater crabs are found throughout the country.

While many insects play important roles as pollinators, or biological controls in gardens and fields, many others spread disease, attack crops, or otherwise cause annoyance. Mosquitoes, flies, and biting gnats are found throughout the country. Fleas, ticks, lice, and roaches are common pests throughout the lowlands. Insect-borne diseases are becoming increasingly widespread. Malaria, as well as diarrhea and other diseases associated with contaminated water supplies, are becoming increasingly severe and widespread. They contribute significantly to the declining life expectancy of Afghans, which currently is one of the world's shortest.

Nomads, such as these shown here, are sharply declining in number as they give up their wandering lifestyle to settle in Afghan towns and cities.

CHAPTER

3

Early History and Culture

Afghanistan has a long and complex history. Without an understanding of the country's past, it is impossible to understand many conditions existing today. For that reason, three chapters are devoted to the topic. This chapter will discuss the country's earliest peoples and their way of life up to the 15th century. Chapter 4, "The Age of European Imperialism," covers the period from the 19th century to the 1970s, during which European influence was strongly imprinted on Afghanistan. Finally, Chapter 5 discusses the country's recent history and the impact of the Soviet invasion.

Prehistory

Ancient Paleolithic (Old Stone Age) people probably roamed what is now Afghanistan as early as 100,000 years ago. Certainly Mousterian (Neanderthal) populations were present in the area

50,000 to 30,000 years ago, during the Middle Paleolithic (Middle Stone Age). Among the archaeological sites yielding evidence of Middle Paleolithic Mousterian occupation are Dara-e Kur in Badakhshan Province and Ghar-e Mordeh Gusfand in Ghowr Province. The Middle Paleolithic was a period during which accumulated knowledge grew rapidly. People learned to make better tools and weapons that, in turn, made it possible for them to exploit a broad range of plant and animal resources. One of their most important tools was fire. This, combined with more effective weapons, contributed to the extinction of many species. The environment, too, underwent change as a result of the widespread use of fire as a hunting and clearing tool. Many wooded areas were changed into the grass-lands that cover widespread areas of Afghanistan even today.

Afghanistan is located within the region of the world that is most often associated with the beginning of the Neolithic (New Stone Age) Revolution. Surprisingly, perhaps, this revolution, although bearing the name "stone," is more involved with the dawn of plant and animal domestication. When domestication first occurred in the region perhaps some 11,000 years ago, people were able to raise crops and tend herds, rather than gathering and hunting to provide their needs. Baluchistan was a particularly important early center of cereal cultivation. The crops included two types of barley, two kinds of wheat, and dates. The resultant crop and livestock combinations allowed societies to control their food supplies. A greater and more reliable food supply also eventually contributed to the emergence of the earliest urban centers, such as Mundigak and Deh Morasi Ghundai near Kandahar. The cultural geographer can learn much by studying early peoples. As the environment changed, society itself changed in many ways. And the transition from rural, nomadic living to city life required a completely different set of social, economic, technological, and other "survival" skills.

With farming and grazing, Afghanistan's environmental

systems began to change. Specifically, they were changed to serve the needs of people and societies that had abandoned hunting and gathering and become involved in agriculture, trade, and other more sedentary forms of livelihood. Grasslands and woodlands were converted to agricultural fields, and open grasslands became pasturelands for domesticated livestock. Grazing livestock, agricultural expansion, and the use of wood for construction and fuel further greatly reduced natural vegetative cover.

Afghanistan provides the environmental geographer with an extensive "laboratory" in which to study the human impact on the natural environment. As natural vegetation cover decreased as a result of human activity, for example, the atmospheric moisture available for precipitation decreased (because of reduced plant transpiration). With reduced vegetation, soil temperatures increased; soil-moisture content was altered; soil ecology was simplified; and soil structure was modified. The foregoing list of changes may seem extremely complex—and it is. However, it illustrates how very complicated natural systems can be, and how a single human act—in this case, reducing natural vegetation cover—can affect other environmental elements. In this example, the quality of soil declined greatly. In fact, conditions favorable for the regeneration of many of Afghanistan's soils and native plants may no longer exist. Agricultural productivity has been reduced, as has the quality of grazing lands. And reduced moisture infiltration and unobstructed runoff have increased flooding that, in turn, affects settlement and other land use activities in the flood-prone lowlands.

Ancient History

Historically, Afghanistan was the meeting place of three major ecological and cultural areas: Central Asia to the north, the Indian Subcontinent to the east, and the Middle East to the west. Located between these centers of powerful civilizations, Afghanistan often fell prey to outside forces. During the mid-first millennium B.C.E., the region became the home of important Eastern Iranian kingdoms, such as Bactria; and it was incorporated into the Achaemenid Empire of the Western Iranians during the sixth century B.C.E.

By the first millennium B.C.E., agriculture and other forms of environmental alteration had been practiced in the region for thousands of years. Erosion, caused by the removal of vegetation, soil compaction, and salinization was severe. Good farmland was reduced, and surface water quality was affected. Many formerly productive lowland basin lakes, such as Namakzar, became *playas*—unproductive desert basins that occasionally hold water. While water from canals and near-surface wells continued to support cultivation in many areas, the deterioration of water quality in other areas encouraged the excavation of underground canals, or *karez*. In northern Afghanistan, they may date from the fifth century B.C.E. It is believed that they were excavated by members of an itinerant guild of specialists. A mid-nineteenth century traveler, Evliya Efendi, wrote:

> The aqueduct-men by their skill in mathematics dig through mountains to the depth of seventy or eighty yards, and conduct the water four or five journies distance. Every hundred paces they open a well-mouth, over which they put a windsail to admit air to the water, till it arrives at the place they desire it to be brought to, by levelling. It is a wonderful art. These men dig here and there, and feign to be consulting from whence water shall be brought, or to where it shall be con-ducted. They are all Albanese.

Most karez are horizontal wells that tap the groundwater from springs that occur in distant alluvial fans found at the base of mountains. Water is then transported (by gravity flow) in underground aqueducts (canals) to an agricultural village. This technology had many applications in the past. In some instances, karez were fed by diverted streams and carried the

Ancient horizontal irrigation tunnels, or karez, still exist and efforts are being made to reactivate the underground system.

water underground to its destination. The karez were able to deliver large quantities of uncontaminated water to upslope soils unaffected by salinization, waterlogging, or flooding. Temples often received water from particular streams considered to be sacred. The karez digging guilds were also called upon occasionally to divert water from cities under siege.

In the semiarid lowlands of Afghanistan, pastoral nomadism emerged from village-based pastoralism. The increased range of livestock grazing permitted the exploitation of increasingly sparse vegetation over vast areas. As environmental systems became less productive, many nomads joined settled Afghan populations in an increasing number of towns and cities—a trend that continues to the present day.

Hellenistic (Greek) influences intensified in Afghanistan following Alexander III of Macedon's (Alexander the Great) victory over the Achaemenid emperor Darius III in 331 B.C.E. and the emergence of the Seleucid Empire. The Seleucid period in Afghanistan is complex, owing to considerable conflict, displacement, and political change. Among the most prominent groups were Greco-Bactrians; the Mauryan Empire under Ashoka (296-237 B.C.E.); the nomadic Saka (Scythians); and the Yüeh-chih (or Kushan nomads). Much of the turmoil ended with the expansion of the Parthian Empire under Mithradates I around 171 B.C.E. It was a powerful empire that prevented further eastward expansion of the Roman Empire.

Afghanistan was also the home of important elements of the later Sassanian Empire, such as the Hephthalites. As the influence of Sassanian kings yielded to the competing interests of religious leaders and bureaucrats, the empire declined. The void was filled by the arrival of Islam, and a succession of extensive Arab caliphates (a successor of Muhammad as a spiritual leader of Islam) that began in 652 A.D.

The Early Islamic Period

Islam reached Afghanistan during the mid-seventh century. Turmoil, however, would persist as control continued to change hands frequently. With the decline of the Abbasid Caliphate in the ninth century A.D., Afghanistan fell under the control of the Tahirid Emirate, and later the Saffarid Emirate. During the 10th century, it was associated with the powerful

Samanid and Ghaznavid Emirates—the latter an indigenous (native) dynasty established by Nasir ad-Dawlah Subuktigin, a Turkish general who overthrew his Samanid master in 977 A.D. Under the leadership of his son, Yamin ad-Dawlah Mahmud, the Ghaznavids created an empire extending from Kurdistan to Kashmir, and from the Amu Darya (Oxus River of antiquity) to the Ganges River. Mahmud was a patron of the arts and litera-ture and was said to have had 900 resident scholars, including the scientist-historian al-Biruni and the poet Firdousi, in his House of Learning.

Afghanistan was later incorporated into the extensive Seljuk Sultanate. Divisions formed within the sultanate, resulting in the emergence of a separate Seljuk Sultanate of Merv in Central Asia. It, in turn, fell into anarchy upon the revolt of its Ghuzz mercenaries. During the 13th century, Afghanistan was included in the Shahdom of Khwarezm, a state then devastated by the merciless campaigns of Genghis Khan and the Mongols in 1220 and 1221. During the 14th century, Mongol authority in Afghanistan yielded to several native provincial governments, such as the Kart Emirate, and they to the forces of the Turkish noble, Timur (Tamburlaine). Effective Timurid control extended through the 15th century.

Cultural Contributions of Early Afghanistan

The many kingdoms and empires that controlled the region at various times made important contributions to reli-gion, literature, architecture, agriculture, gardening, and crafts.

It was from this region that the prophet Zoroaster (ca. 628–ca. 551 B.C.E.) introduced the strict dualism of good and evil principles, light and dark, and angels and devils that so profoundly influenced Hebrew beliefs, Greek thought, and Christianity. It was also from Afghanistan, chiefly from the first through the fifth centuries A.D., that Mahayana Buddhism traveled eastward over the ancient Silk Route to Mongolia, China, Korea, and Japan. (Ironically, the Buddhist Mongol

Hordes of Genghis Khan followed the same route westward in the 1220 and 1221 campaigns that ravaged Afghanistan.) Since the arrival of Islam, Afghanistan has been associated with Sufi mysticism—a vehicle for seeking God through personal experience and achieving momentary union with God. Among the well-known Afghan Sufis were Sana'i (died 1150) of Ghazni and Rumi (1207–1273), born in Balkh and founder of the Mawlawiya Dervishes.

Herat, Balkh, Kabul, and Ghazni were prominent literary centers in Afghanistan. The court compositions of the Achaemenid Empire (559–30 B.C.E.) established literary traditions echoed in later works, such as the *Shahname* (Book of Kings) by Firdousi (died ca. 1020 A.D.). Firdousi was the most prominent of the 400 poets who resided in the court of Mahmud of Ghazni. The *Shahname* ranks among the world's great epic poems.

In addition to the more or less official manuals of the imperial court, there were historical romances, urban histories, and compilations concerned with ethics. But the region is best known for its excellent poetry. Much of the poetry was of considerable length—the *Shahname*, for example, was composed of 60,000 rhyming couplets. That of the mathematician and philosopher Omar Khayyám (died 1123) is representative of a shorter verse-form, the popular *ruba'i*:

> A Book of Verses underneath the Bough,
> A Jug of Wine, a Loaf of Bread—and Thou
> Beside me singing in the Wilderness—
> O, Wilderness were Paradise enow!

Prominent among later Afghan authors was Jami (1414–1492), a poet, scholar, and mystic who wrote at least 46 major works in the fields of lyrical and romantic narrative poetry, grammar, music, mysticism, the lives of the Sufi saints, and Koranic studies. In Afghanistan, the mysticism and the polished elegance of Persian poetry later developed in tandem with works in the more direct language of the tribal poets. For them, prowess in warfare against infidel (non-Muslim) foreigners was a favorite theme:

> Whoever is a Moslem, whoever is of good faith in Islam . . . goes to the sacred war, gives up his life and goods for the law of the Holy Prophet, and is not afraid of the infidels.

Other popular themes were love, jealousy, religion, and folklore. Today, most Afghans, literate or nonliterate, consider themselves to be poets—and prior to the Soviet military incursions of the late 1970s, a remarkable literary renaissance was taking place in Afghanistan. It found expression in the many journals and other publications of the Pushtu Tulena (Afghan Academy), the Afghan Encyclopedia Society, the Anjoman Tarikh-e Afghanistan (Afghan Historical Society), and other scholarly societies.

Several architectural innovations were established within the ancient empires of the region—including the arch, barrel-vault, and dome—that strongly influenced the architecture of Greece, Rome, and the modern world. Among the oldest excavated sites in Afghanistan is a temple complex at Sorkh Kowtal, located between Baghlan and Pol-e Khomri in ancient Bactria. It consists of a principal temple and a *cella* (square area marked by four column bases). A secondary temple leans against the exterior wall of the main temple and contains a square fire altar (Zoroastrian). A staircase of monumental proportions reaches from top to bottom of the high hill-temple complex, connecting four distinct terraced embankments. The massive horizontal (waterwheel) water-mills of Afghanistan, often associated with karez, are also remnants of ancient architectural traditions. Also of interest is the pigeon tower. These large, ornate towers attract and house pigeons; the droppings are collected and used for fertilizer and in tanning leather.

Pigeons were housed in ancient Afghanistan, and droppings were collected and used for fertilizer and in tanning leather.

From its very beginning, perhaps 11,000 years ago, the agricultural systems of Afghanistan have been the most important aspect of the country's society and economy. Elements of the ancient systems are described in the *Geoponika,* a book on agriculture written by ancient Greek and Roman scholars. The agricultural population included sedentary farmers, semi-sedentary farmers, seminomads, and nomads. These groups were both interdependent and occasionally in conflict. Among the land tenure systems associated with sedentary farmers were those controlled by landlords. In them, agricultural production typically involved five elements: land, water, seed, animal power, and human labor. Whoever contributed one of the elements received one-fifth of the crop. Land and water rights were linked and were owned by the landlord. The landlord would typically provide the seed; animal traction might be contributed by the landlord or villagers; and the villagers provided the labor. Those who actually worked the land would typically receive one-fifth to two-fifths of the crop.

The English word "paradise" came from the Persian word *pairidaeza* used in reference to Persian gardens. It is said that a Persian ruler so admired the royal gardens of the Lydian Empire in Anatolia (present-day Turkey), that he established similar gardens throughout the Achaemenid Empire (including in Afghanistan). The gardens were (and still are in some locations) on a grand scale. They typically include combinations of trees, shrubs, and flowers, as well as watercourses and fountains. The garden is designed to provide aesthetic pleasure. It will have a variety of sweet scents, comfortably cool temperatures during the summer, a variety of fruits and flowers, and a habitat to attract birds. The gardens of Kandahar and several other urban centers in Afghanistan were well known in the past.

Despite the sophisticated metallurgy and other crafts associated with the region, Afghanistan, like Iran, is particularly well known for its beautiful carpets—a tradition of craftsmanship known for more than 2,500 years. Today, most Afghan carpets are of the Buxoro (Bukhara), or Turkoman type, characterized by parallel rows of geometric figures on a dark red field. Most highly regarded are carpets woven in Faryab Province. Additional Afghan contributions were made in the areas of philosophy, logic, medicine, mathematics, astronomy, music, and mechanics. With the arrival of Islam, the region also became a center of scholastic theology, jurisprudence, poetry, and historical scholarship.

The entrance to the Soviet-built Salang Tunnel through the Hindu Kush mountains is shown here.

4

The Age of European Imperialism

During the 16th and 17th centuries, the Persian Safavids and Indian Mughals (Moghuls) unsuccessfully attempted to control Afghanistan. In 1747 the last great Afghan empire rose under the leadership of Ahmad Shah Durrani of Kandahar. The 19th century witnessed tribal conflicts and the intrusion of European imperialism (controlling influence) into the area. Afghanistan became a battleground in the rivalry between Great Britain and czarist Russia for control of Central Asia. Two Anglo-Afghan Wars (1839-1842 and 1878-1880) ended inconclusively. After the second Anglo-Afghan War, the British supported Abdur Rahman Khan's claim to the Afghan throne. Then, with British arms, the "Iron Amir" (1880-1901) subdued rebellious Pashtuns, as well as other, formerly autonomous, tribal groups and successfully consolidated the

Afghan state. Some observers claim that much of Afghanistan's recent tribal conflict can be traced to Abdur Rahman's policies that were implemented more than a century ago.

In 1893, Great Britain established an unofficial border, the Durand Line, which separated Afghanistan from British India, and separated ethnically related tribal groups as well. From a British perspective, Afghanistan was both a buffer between its Indian colony and czarist Russia, and an element of a more ambitious objective—clear global dominance. This objective prompted numerous 19th-century exploratory expeditions and was later expressed in British geographer Sir Halford Mackinder's "Heartland Theory." This theory was first expressed in 1904 and was greatly expanded upon in his book, *Democratic Ideas and Reality*, published in 1919. Mackinder believed that it was important to control the interior of Eurasia, an area he called the "heartland," part of the "World Island." His state-ment, which had a profound impact on political geography and the military policy of many countries, read:

> Who rules East Europe commands the Heartland
> Who rules the Heartland commands the World Island;
> Who rules the World Island commands the World.

Similar sentiments were expressed by Lord Curzon, who was the British Viceroy of India from 1898 to 1905:

> Turkistan, Afghanistan, Transcaspia, Persia—to many these words breathe only a sense of utter remoteness or a memory of strange vicissitudes and moribund romance. To me, I confess they are the pieces on a chessboard upon which is being played out a game for the dominance of the World.

Pronouncements such as those made by Mackinder and Curzon clearly help to explain Britain's interest in the region. Once again, Afghanistan was a pawn in someone else's game of power and control.

Independence

Following the third Anglo-Afghan War in 1919, Afghanistan gained full control over its foreign affairs under the conditions of the Treaty of Rawalpindi. The country thus became fully independent. In 1921 an Afghan-Soviet treaty of friendship was signed, further reducing outside pressures on the country.

King Amanullah

Emir Amanullah founded an Afghan monarchy in 1926 and undertook a tour of several Middle Eastern and European countries. He returned to Kabul eager to promote European concepts regarding social change and economic development. He decreed that women should go unveiled in Kabul and that men should wear European clothing. He presented his ideas to a traditional council, a *Loya Jirgeh*. Most of the participants were strongly attached to the traditional way of life and sided with the Muslim religious leaders and tribal elements strongly opposed to these foreign innovations. In 1928 the Shinwari Pashtun gained control of Jalalabad and the Tajik Habibullah Ghazi (better known as Bacheh Saqqo) assembled his followers to the north of Kabul. The forces of Bacheh Saqqo attacked the outskirts of Kabul in December 1928, and in January 1929 Amanullah abdicated in favor of his older brother, Inayatullah, and fled to Kandahar hoping to recruit tribesmen loyal to him and regain the throne. Inayatullah ruled for three days before Bacheh Saqqo entered the capital, proclaimed himself emir, or ruler, and revoked the initiatives of Amanullah. The Soviets, who had supported Amanullah's efforts in modernization, were convinced that the British had backed Bacheh Saqqo and took active steps

Nadir Shah was proclaimed ruler, and his coronation took place in November 1929. He was assassinated four years later.

to restore Amanullah to the throne. However, they were unsuccessful in doing so.

Nadir Shah

Members of the powerful Musahiban family gathered tribal elements and gained control of Kabul in October

1929. Nadir Khan was proclaimed ruler; his coronation as Nadir Shah took place in November. He restored order throughout the country; abandoned the emphasis upon rapid modernization; promoted economic development; and was responsible for the drafting of the 1931 constitution —a somewhat conservative version of Amanullah's 1923 constitution. In November 1933, Nadir Shah was assassinated by a supporter of Amanullah, and his eldest son, Muhammad Zahir, succeeded to the throne at 19 years of age.

Muhammad Zahir

Although Muhammad Zahir had become king, the affairs of state were initially in the hands of his uncles, Muhammad Hashim, who served as prime minister from 1933 to 1946, and Shah Mahmud, who served as prime minister until 1953—at which time his cousin, Sirdar (Prince) Muhammad Daoud Khan, became prime minister through a bloodless coup d'état.

Under the leadership of Muhammad Hashim, Afghanistan ended its policy of isolation, foreign trade was expanded, and many schools were constructed. While essentially neutral during World War II, Afghanistan honored the request by the British and Soviets to expel all nationals of the Axis nations (countries supporting Germany and Italy in World War II) who did not enjoy diplomatic status. This decision halted the delivery of equipment and the construction of several new factories being developed with German assistance. In 1946, immediately after the end of World War II, Afghanistan took another major step in becoming more involved in the global community when it joined the United Nations (UN).

In subsequent years, under Shah Mahmud, the Afghans promoted the creation of an independent *Pashtunistan.* Their goal was to eventually reunite Pashtun tribesmen

King Muhammad Zahir Shah was exiled to Italy after the monarchy was overthrown by forces organized by Muhammad Daoud in 1973.

separated by the Durand Line. They also sought to shift from the encouragement of private enterprise to state control over finance, commerce, and industry; engage in economic development financed largely by foreign grants and loans; and ostensibly to maintain a foreign policy of nonalignment (neutrality in conflicts involving other countries). The government of Shah Mahmud also developed the Helmand Valley Authority (HVA) launched by his predecessor. The HVA was an ambitious river-basin development project regulated by high dams on the Helmand and Arghandab Rivers.

The Decade of Daoud Khan

The foreign policy of Shah Mahmud had favored the West, rather than maintaining traditional Afghan neutrality. In the early 1950s, frustrated by little progress with regard to the creation of Pashtunistan, increased American aid to Pakistan, and the apparent lack of American interest in Afghan problems, Daoud seized control of the government. Also among Daoud's concerns were issues related to the HVA. The project was designed to permit the cultivation of two grain crops annually. Instead, owing to salinization, waterlogging, and other problems, crop yields declined by 50 percent, or even more in some areas. Because an engineering firm from the United States designed the project, the failure affected Afghan trust in American technical assistance.

Daoud's government moved closer to the Soviet Union to restore balance in foreign affairs and to profit from Cold War competition between the two superpowers. As in the past, the Soviets actively promoted modernization. State-planned efforts in economic development were promoted. Soviet technicians, including petroleum geologists, seismic engineers, veterinarians, agricultural specialists, and others, actively participated in exploration for petroleum, the construction of factories, the expansion of telephone and telegraph lines, and a variety of agricultural projects. Laws were passed permitting freedom of the press, and various student movements flourished.

The unwillingness of the United States to support the

construction of a road connecting Afghanistan with the port of Chabahar in Iran on the Arabian Sea further encouraged cooperation with the Soviet Union. The road would have eliminated the necessity of transporting goods through Pakistan, thus separating considerations of trade from the issue of Pashtunistan. It would have permitted access to established markets in India, the Middle East, and Europe, rather than having to create new markets in the Soviet Union. The Soviets responded with commodity-exchange arrangements, such as the exchange of petroleum and building materials for Afghan wool, raw cotton, and hides. A major Soviet loan then resulted in the construction of many facilities. These included two hydroelectric plants; the improvement of automotive maintenance and repair facilities; the construction of roads, bridges, and the Salang Tunnel (a two-mile long tunnel, the world's highest, through the Hindu Kush range north of Kabul); the improvement of port facilities at Shir Khan (on the Amu Darya); airport construction; irrigation dams and canals; a materials-testing laboratory; and a fertilizer factory. The projects also served Soviet self-interest. As Nikita Khrushchev noted in his memoirs, *Khrushchev Remembers:*

> There's no doubt that if the Afghans hadn't become our friends, the Americans would have managed to ingratiate themselves with their "humanitarian aid," as they call it. The amount of money we spent in gratuitous assistance to Afghanistan is a drop in the ocean compared to the price we would have had to pay in order to counter the threat of an American military base on Afghan territory.

As usual during the Cold War, increased American aid followed Soviet aid and grew steadily as Daoud exploited competition between the two superpowers.

Soviet inroads into Afghanistan rekindled memories of

the efforts of czarist Russia to expand southward to the warm waters of the Arabian Sea and Persian Gulf. To counter these inroads, Americans offered assistance motivated by efforts to "contain Communism" and to develop joint military pacts to halt "Communist aggression." In its efforts to contain Communism, the United States established several treaty organizations that joined together a number of countries that would support America's political interests in the region. These alliances included the Southeast Asia Treaty Organization (SEATO), the Central Treaty Organization (CENTO); and the North Atlantic Treaty Organization (NATO).

Nevertheless, the Soviet Union and the United States continued their efforts to gain favor with the Afghans through investment in high-profile assistance projects. When the Export-Import Bank turned down a 1953 Afghan request to pave Kabul's streets, the Soviets assisted in paving them. When, in 1956, the Afghans proposed Kandahar as a pivotal center for air traffic in the Middle East-South Asia corridor, the United States constructed the Kandahar International Airport. Some American assistance was extended with genuine concern for the well-being of its recipients. But many of its grants and loans were typically linked to the American need for strong allies, for military bases on foreign soil, or for the control of strategic resources.

The Soviet Union, on the other hand, claimed to provide extensive aid to other countries without imposing terms incompatible with their national interests and dignity. They boasted that there were never military or political strings attached to their aid. In reality, however, the Soviets believed that it was unnecessary to attach military and political strings, because economic penetration was the easiest and most logical way to influence all institutions in a society. Despite claims of social sensitivity, Soviet policy was devastating to the affected societies in Central Asia. In his book *Afghanistan*, Louis Dupree writes:

> Generally, the removal of indigenous Muslim religious leaders accelerated forced collectivization or industrialization. After Russification had taken root and religion had been successfully deemphasized, especially in its ritual [and] symbolic aspects, the Soviets often permitted Communist-sanitized Islam to exist. Communist theorists concluded political Communism can be made compatible with any form of religion through a shift in economic patterns and the removal of religiously oriented vested interest groups.

Soviet efforts in promoting modernization marginalized Afghan traditionalists. It also understandably conflicted with the beliefs of many Afghan religious leaders. These two miscalculations eventually were major factors leading to the collapse of the Soviet Union. The approach taken by the Soviets is somewhat similar to later American policies involving the expansion of market economies and the forceful removal of the country's ruling Taliban government. The point is not a matter of "right" or "wrong"; rather, it is one of a foreign power imposing its will on Afghanistan's people, economy, and government.

The United States and the Soviet Union were not the only countries active in Afghanistan. Diplomatic relations had been established with many countries during the reign of Amanullah. It was within the context of increasingly complex international relationships that the Afghans attempted to understand their relationship with the United States. Dupree writes:

> The seeming inconsistencies in United States foreign policy, however, puzzled Afghans, as well as many

Americans. Some Afghans cannot understand why the United States and the Soviet Union, staunch allies in World War II, became post-war antagonists so quickly. Conversely, the United States alignment with West Germany and Japan, former blood enemies, runs counter to the Afghan concept of loyalty. American policies with regard to Israel, the Arab States, Kashmir, and "P[a]shtunistan" also baffle the Afghans. Beyond all comprehension were the American frantic efforts to bring neutral nations into military regional pacts.

Further attempts were made to secure American arms. However, American policy required that weapons provided by the United States be used only to resist "aggression." From an Afghan perspective, it was not clear what was considered to be aggression, or who was to define it. For example, Afghans considered the French to be aggressors in Algeria and political Zionists to be aggressors in Palestine—whereas the French and Americans viewed the relationships quite differently. Further, American airplanes and weapons were used to subdue Pashtun "rebels" in Pakistan. It is often difficult to identify the aggressor in a civil war, a revolution, or action taken against an unjust regime.

Failing to secure military assistance from the United States, the Afghans obtained small arms, tanks, fighter aircraft, bombers, and helicopters from the Soviet Union, Czechoslovakia, Poland, Hungary, and East Germany. The Soviets also assisted in the construction of military airfields near Mazar-e Sharif, Bagram, and Shindand. At the time, both Washington and Moscow assumed that the provision of military support implied alliance and, in this case, the U.S. Army believed that Afghanistan had "gone Communist." In fact, the Afghans still regarded themselves as being non-aligned. As Daoud commented:

Our whole life, our whole existence, revolves around one single focal point—freedom. Should we ever get the feeling that our freedom is in the slightest danger, from whatever quarter, then we should prefer to live on dry bread, or even starve, sooner than accept help that would restrict our freedom.

In the early 1960s, the exclusive competition between the Americans and Soviets in Afghanistan effectively ended. Both countries became actively involved in technical-assistance projects throughout the country and both provided military training for Afghan officers. While the United States and the Soviet Union both hoped to gain an ally and counter the moves of the other, the Afghans saw little difference between the two. Their relationships with the Soviet Union and the United States tended to reinforce Afghan nationalism, while serving the government's efforts in modernization.

Purdah and the *Chadri*

The government of King Amanullah fell in 1929 because it abolished *purdah* and the *chadri* and established coeducational schools in Kabul. Nonetheless, the government of Daoud initiated similar measures in modernization. Purdah is a system in certain Muslim and Hindu societies of screening women from strangers. The chadri is a sack-like garment of pleated, colored silk or rayon, which covers the entire body from head to toe. An embroidered latticework covers the eyes and permits limited vision. Prior to taking these steps toward modernization the Daoud government carefully examined the Koran; the Hadith, which is the record of the sayings of Muhammad; and the Hanafi Sharia of Sunni Islam, which is a school of Islamic law. It found no mention of a requirement for either purdah or the wearing of a chadri.

It was clear that Islam, as a faith, did not regard women as being inferior to men. Historically, Muslim women have played

Women wearing the chadri shop for clothing at a roadside market in Kabul.

important roles in social, political, and economic matters. In fact, the customs of purdah and the chadri also were associated with wealthy, urbanized Christian and Zoroastrian women in the lands of the Byzantine and Sassanian empires conquered by the Arabs in the seventh century A.D. It appears that purdah and the chadri were adopted by nomadic Arab women in part because doing so conferred the perceived status of the urban women of the civilizations conquered. Many other factors also may have been involved in its adoption, including that chadri put all women in public on an equal basis; the customs provided protection for women during periods of political instability; and the customs entered Afghanistan with the arrival of Islam. Further, as do many cultures, those of the Middle East attach importance to complementary "inward" and "outward" gender relationships—with women controlling the inward world of the home and family; whereas men are responsible for interaction with the world beyond the home. Adoption of purdah and the chadri helped to reinforce these relationships.

Perhaps the most outspoken opposition to the abolition of purdah and the chadri came from Muslim clerics. They accused the government of abandoning Islam in favor of the values of atheistic Communism and the Christian West. They realized that many aspects of urban popular culture, including the cinema, music, and less formal social relationships, were attractive to some people—particularly the young. These foreign influences, they realized, posed a great threat to traditional Afghan culture. Kandahar was, and remains, a center of religious conservatism. As with the later Taliban, resistance to the new policies emerged most dramatically in Kandahar with the riots of 1959.

The issue of Pashtunistan continued to surface, and its creation was strongly supported by the Daoud government. Pakistan, now allied with the United States, strongly opposed the creation of a Pashtunistan. Violence erupted on both sides of the border and, in 1961, Afghan troops advanced across the border. While the Afghans were successful in conventional warfare, they were no match for Pakistan's jet fighter planes. Rather than becoming involved in a full-scale war, the conflict devolved into occasional skirmishes and a continuing war of words.

Outside viewers often forget that in Middle Eastern countries—largely creations of European policy or convenience—relationships are often driven more by ethnicity than by national identity. Indeed, in some instances, divisions *within* ethnic groups can play an important role. For example, Pashtun tribes often fought each other. Sometimes tribes would ally themselves with either Afghanistan or Pakistan in search of greater support and favor. On occasion, all Pashtun tribes would unite in opposition to Pakistan. The somewhat arbitrary creation of countries by Europeans simply added a variable that could be included in local political tribal and ethnic strategies.

At the national level, diplomatic relationships were broken between Afghanistan and Pakistan, and the border was closed. Because Afghanistan is landlocked, its exports traditionally had traveled southward through Pakistan to ports on the Arabian Sea. It was assumed by many that Afghanistan would take into account the economic costs of its stance and relent. Typically, however, Afghan pride overrode practical considerations and it refused to yield. Instead, Afghanistan established even closer economic ties with the Soviet Union to the north, a reality that placed the United States in an awkward position. The United States had allied itself with Pakistan but continued to attach importance to Afghanistan in relation to its strategy of Soviet containment. Pakistan then requested that the United Kingdom represent its interests in Kabul. This proposal was unacceptable to the Afghans, who regarded the British, who had imposed the Durand Line, to be the ultimate culprit in the difficulties that they were experiencing. Further, as one Afghan intellectual commented, "The British are using America to reassert themselves in Asia. America is still a British colony whether it chooses to believe it or not." (Dupree, 1973) This important period in Afghan history came to an end with the abrupt resignation of Prime Minister Daoud in 1963.

The Constitutional Period

Although Daoud had served the country well as its prime minister, many people were pleased with his resignation. Some hoped that the border with Pakistan would reopen, permitting normal trade relations to the south. Pashtun nomads hoped that they could again follow traditional migratory routes—routes that had been cut off by closure of the border. Residents of Kabul anticipated a greater availability of consumer goods and reduced prices. Socially conservative Afghans looked forward to a return to traditional values, as Daoud had agreed to all Soviet initiatives in modernization. They particularly resented initiatives that altered the status of women in society. Civil servants, professionals, and students looked forward to increased emphasis upon social and political reforms that had been neglected during the Pashtunistan crisis. Americans and Germans were pleased, owing to the belief that their equipment and commercial goods might soon reach Afghanistan through Pakistan. Iranians hoped to claim some credit for their efforts in promoting better relations between Afghanistan and Pakistan. And Pakistan was pleased with the anticipated reduction of tension along the border and normalized trade.

Other Afghans were uncomfortable with Daoud's resignation—particularly supporters of Pashtunistan. Members of the royal family were concerned by a possible erosion of their authority in the affairs of government; many military officers and intellectuals were committed to their country's ongoing relationship with the Soviet Union.

With Daoud's departure, Muhammad Zahir Shah firmly grasped the reins of government. Although he had reigned for 30 years, the affairs of government had been in the hands of his uncles and his cousin, Daoud. He now ruled. The king then separated the royal family from the executive branch of government, preparing the way for the formation of a constitutional monarchy. Daoud was replaced as prime minister by Muhammad Yousuf, who had served as minister of mines and industries. Policies under Yousuf differed little from those of his predecessor, although there was a somewhat greater emphasis on private enterprise, the need for constitutional reform, and efforts to establish a more representative system of government.

Several measures first initiated by Daoud's government were realized: the value of Afghan currency was stabilized with support from the International Monetary Fund; the Soviet Union and the United States agreed to undertake new road projects; Ariana Afghan Airlines purchased new aircraft in the United States and expanded its services; the American Peace Corps became actively involved in Afghanistan; and the United States committed the funds necessary to complete the construction of Kabul University. Freedom of the press was also expanded and prison reforms were initiated. In the past, Afghan prisons had emphasized punishment rather than rehabilitation, and prisoners were often shackled and beaten. In May 1963, the Iranian government invited Afghan and Pakistani delegations to Tehran. It successfully negotiated the restoration of diplomatic and trade relations between the two former enemies. Finally, the most important accomplishment of the government was the introduction of a new constitution in 1964. The constitution was believed by many to be the finest in the Muslim world. With its acceptance, Afghanistan became a hereditary constitutional monarchy.

Despite a continuing presence in Afghanistan during the 1960s, the energies of the United States were increasingly diverted by its involvement in the Vietnam War. As Joseph Collins wrote in *The Soviet Invasion of Afghanistan* (1986):

> [During this period] Soviet economic aid continued along with Soviet developmental assistance, in spite of its aggregate decrease in value during the Vietnam War, hitting 70 percent of total Afghan aid during the period 1967-70. This was in marked contrast to the United States whose aid during this period dipped temporarily from one-third of total Afghan aid in 1967 to less than 3 percent of the total in 1969. By 1973, total Soviet military and economic aid ($1.5 billion) outweighed U.S. economic aid ($425 million) by a factor of three to one.

Although by 1967 the Afghan armed forces had become almost wholly dependent upon the Soviets, Afghans were often critical of Soviet policy and attempted to maintain their nonaligned status.

While the 1964 constitution addressed a broad range of important issues, its promotion of modernization offended many traditionalists. Further, the king discouraged the long-term development of political parties, and the separation of powers within the government was extreme. The prime minister was responsible to the king, but had little influence over the Parliament. The king himself exercised little leadership, hoping that the system would function effectively of its own accord. Finally, members of the royal family were no longer permitted to participate in political parties or to hold the following offices: prime minister or minister, member of Parliament, or justice of the Supreme Court. Because the day-to-day operation of the government had been in the hands of the royal family for decades, governance fell into less experienced hands. Daoud and other individuals who could have contributed became disaffected. Further, the pace of social change was disorienting to many people. Urban growth was accompanied by accelerated modernization. Expanded educational opportunity resulted in a dramatic increase in high school and university graduates, but employment opportunities were limited. Finally, the country had no planning program, a poorly developed banking system, and no civil service.

There was rapid turnover in government officials. Student protests erupted, and their often-violent suppression alienated many students. In an October 1965 demonstration, Afghan troops fired upon student protesters, leaving three dead and several wounded. Student-worker protests occurred in 1968; policemen quelling a demonstration in the spring of 1969 killed several students; and student protests once again erupted in 1971. The initial protests were largely nonideological. Increasingly, however, both alienated politicians and frustrated students sought solutions by more radical political means.

The People's Democratic Party of Afghanistan (PDPA), led by Nur Muhammad Taraki and Babrak Karmal, became a vehicle for opposition to the government. Taraki was a well-known liberal intellectual who had been a government bureaucrat and a translator for the American diplomatic mission. Karmal had served in the government and had twice been elected to the Parliament. The party sought to establish a socialist society that adapted Marxist-Leninist principles to conditions in Afghanistan.

The Return of Daoud Khan

The results of the elections of 1969 revealed that Afghan tribal leaders, who were both socially and religiously conservative, had developed a better understanding of the electoral process. In the election they gained control of the Parliament. They did so with the goal of preserving traditional values and limiting further efforts in modernization. Following his departure from Afghan politics in 1963, Daoud had conducted an ongoing discussion with army officers and political activists. By this dialogue, he hoped to assess the strengths and weaknesses of his regime (1953-1963) and what might be done to solve the problems of contemporary Afghanistan. Dissatisfied with the directions taken in Afghan politics since his departure, Daoud, with support from the army and the palace guard, overthrew the monarchy in 1973. Muhammad Zahir Shah, at the time vacationing in Italy, was exiled. His family later joined him.

Daoud immediately made many changes in the way the country was governed. He established a military government; he reaffirmed his commitment to basic Islamic principles; his policy of nonalignment was reiterated; and he promised to seek a peaceful resolution of the Pashtunistan issue. Among other tasks, Daoud strengthened the army and the institutions of government; he further expanded Afghanistan's relationship with the Soviet Union; and he attempted to develop an

Following his 1973 takeover of the government, Muhammad Daoud was named president and began the modernization of Afghanistan.

industrial sector that would replace agriculture and handicrafts as the principal sources of wealth in the country. Through industrialization, Daoud hoped to generate a broad base of popular support within Afghanistan. He hoped to eventually lead the country into greater political and economic independence. If this was to be accomplished, he had to have the means to more aggressively pursue future efforts toward modernization. To achieve these ends, he introduced a new constitution in 1977 that banned all political parties other than his own—the National Revolutionary Party. The Republic of Afghanistan was then formally established; Daoud was proclaimed president. He also assumed responsibility for defense and foreign affairs.

Resistance to Daoud's policies surfaced almost immediately. Some Kabul-based groups believed that the pace of modernization was too deliberate. More conservative groups in rural areas felt that modernization should be abandoned altogether. It was at this time that militant tribal leaders, the *mujaheddin*, entered Afghan politics. Armed and trained by Pakistan, mujaheddin leaders, including Gulbuddin Hikmetyar, Burhanuddin Rabbani, and Ahmad Shah Masud, attacked politically sensitive targets in an effort to undermine the Daoud government. Many urban political activists who were supported by the Soviets represented an even greater threat to Daoud, who attempted to purge these elements from both the military and government. In response, many of the same elements of the army that had brought him to power in 1973 overthrew him in a bloody military coup in 1978. In this so-called Saur Revolution, Daoud, his family, and the presidential guard were all killed. This event ushered in still another turbulent era in Afghanistan's history.

Afghan guerrillas were ready to fight for their cultural traditions and way of life when the Soviets invaded in 1979.

CHAPTER

5

The Soviet Invasion and Its Aftermath

With the death of Daoud, Nur Muhammad Taraki, the leader of the *Khalq* (the masses) faction of the PDPA, assumed the presidency. Almost immediately, conflict arose between the Khalq and the more moderate *Parcham* (the flag) faction. Further, there was growing resistance in rural communities to the modernization initiatives of the communists. Among the initiatives were land reform, industrialization, and literacy programs, some of which would have benefited rural populations. Hence, while the communist factions were engaged in their own struggle, *mullahs* and *khans* (religious and tribal leaders) declared a *jihad* (holy war) against the communist infidels (non-Muslims). President Taraki was assassinated in 1979, and his Khalq successor, Hafizullah Amin, was killed when 85,000 Soviet troops were dispatched to Kabul in December 1979. Ironically, the troops had been requested by

President Amin. But the Soviets felt that the civil strife created by Khalq policies threatened their influence and investments in Afghanistan, as well as the security of the Soviet republics to the north. They therefore deposed Amin and his supporters and replaced them with Babrak Karmal of the Parcham faction, and his more moderate approach to socialist reform.

With the 1979 Soviet invasion, Afghanistan found itself in the midst of an intensified competition between the Soviet Union and the United States. The conservative mujaheddin were the chief opponents of the Soviets and their Afghan allies. The jihad gained momentum as the United States, China, and Arab states provided the mujaheddin with money, arms, other supplies, and logistical support to partially offset the equivalent of approximately US$45 billion invested by the Soviets in their unsuccessful effort to defeat the mujaheddin. The United States committed roughly $5 billion, a sum matched by Saudi Arabia and other contributors. Most of the aid was in the form of modern weapons. The Ghilzai Pashtun in eastern Afghanistan and around the capital city of Kabul were the chief recipients of aid directed to the mujaheddin; the Durrani Pashtun, located in southern Afghanistan and the Kandahar region, received comparatively little support.

In 1986, Babrak Karmal resigned as president and was replaced by an associate, Muhammad Najibullah. In 1988, the leaders of several Afghan factions formed an interim government in exile based in Pakistan. Faced with broadening Islamic opposition, the economic costs of the Afghanistan conflict, and the political costs of the conflict at home and abroad, the Soviets withdrew their troops in 1989. For most Afghans, the Soviet invasion had simply been another attempt by foreigners to dominate them. The Soviets, as had so many others, had tried to replace Afghan Islamic beliefs and other cultural traditions with an alien ideology and social system.

At a cost of more than 1.5 million Afghan lives—roughly equal to the combined populations of Montana and North

Land mines from earlier conflicts continue to plague the people of Afghanistan. These patients are waiting for treatment at a hospital for mine victims north of Kabul.

Dakota—the mujaheddin and their "Arab Afghan" allies had contributed to one of the most significant events of the 20th century. They played what some observers believe to have been a major role in bringing about the collapse of the Soviet Union and with it, the retreat of international communism. Among the so-called "Arab Afghan" fighters, however, very few were Afghans and relatively few were Arabs. They were composed of volunteers from nearly 60 different countries.

The International Committee of the Red Cross noted that the conflict with the Soviets and its aftermath left 98,000 Afghan families headed by a widow, and 63,000 headed by a disabled person. The conflict and its aftermath also left 500,000 disabled orphans. Many children, as well as adults, were killed or crippled by land mines laid during the 1979-1989 conflict.

This problem was compounded during the 2001-2002 military conflict by the presence of unexploded bombs—particularly cluster bombs. These weapons are attractive to children; they can also be easily mistaken for the yellow food packages dropped from American aircraft.

Owing in part to the destruction of wells, karez, and storage and distribution systems, only 12 percent of the population has access to clean drinking water. The lack of pure water supplies is a major factor contributing to the death of one out of every four children before the age of five—in 2002, the highest rate of infant mortality in the world. Afghanistan's rate for death of women in childbirth is also the highest in the world. Additionally, the conflict destroyed 12,000 of the 22,000 villages in the country, and 2,000 schools. More than six million Afghans sought shelter in Pakistan and Iran, and many remained as refugees during the turbulent years following the Soviet withdrawal. The number of Afghan refugees in Pakistan alone rose from an estimated 18,329 in 1978 to 2,800,000 in 1982.

Armed opposition to the regime of President Najibullah followed the Soviet withdrawal. Najibullah was overthrown in 1992, and the mujaheddin captured Kabul. Much of the subsequent conflict occurred as a result of the fact that Kabul fell not to the well-armed Pashtun factions based in Peshawar, but to the Tajik forces of Burhanuddin Rabbani and his military commander Ahmad Shah Masud, and to the Uzbek forces of Rashid Dostum. It was the first time in 300 years that Pashtuns had lost control of Kabul, and Gulbuddin Hikmetyar rallied Pashtun forces in an attempt to reclaim the city.

Afghanistan itself was virtually fragmented. The country was essentially divided into fiefdoms—small warring states in which factions fought, switched sides, and fought again in a bewildering array of alliances, betrayals, and bloodshed. The largely Tajik government of Rabbani controlled Kabul and northeastern Afghanistan. Dostum, an Uzbek leader, controlled the several northern provinces. The eastern border provinces were controlled by a council of mujaheddin commanders based in Jalalabad. A small region to the southeast of Kabul was under the control of Hikmetyar. In central Afghanistan, the Hazaras controlled the province of Bamian. Much of western Afghanistan was controlled from Herat by Ismael Khan. Southern Afghanistan was divided among several minor mujaheddin leaders and bandits who plundered the population at will. According to Ahmed Rashid in his book, *Taliban*:

> International aid agencies were fearful of even working in Kandahar as the city itself was divided by warring groups. Their leaders sold off everything to Pakistani traders to make money, stripping down telephone wires and poles, cutting trees, selling off factories, machinery and even road rollers to scrap merchants. The warlords seized homes and farms, threw out their occupants and handed them over to their supporters. The commanders abused the population at will, kidnapping young girls and boys for their sexual pleasure, robbing merchants in the bazaars and fighting and brawling in the streets. Instead of refugees returning from Pakistan, a fresh wave of refugees began to leave Kandahar for Quetta.

In 1994, Dostum abandoned his alliance with the Rabbani government and joined with Hikmetyar to attack Kabul. The following conflict led to a second generation of mujaheddin, the Taliban. Because most of those involved in the formation of the Taliban were students at *madrassas*, the name was easily acquired. A *talib* is an Islamic student, or one who seeks knowledge, as opposed to a mullah, or one who imparts knowledge. A madrassa is a school in which the Islamic sciences are taught, but the term may also be applied to any school for students up to age 17 or 18.

The Rise and Fall of the Taliban

Mullah Muhammad Hassan, the governor of Kandahar, described some of the reasons for the formation of the Taliban:

> We all knew each other—Mullahs Omar, Ghaus, Mohammed Rabbani (no relation to President Rabbani) and myself—because we were all originally from Urozgan province and had fought together. I moved back and forth from Quetta and attended *madrassas* there, but whenever we got together we would discuss the terrible plight of our people living under these bandits. We were people of the same opinions and we got on with each other very well, so it was easy to come to a decision to do something. (Rashid, 2000)

The leaders of the Taliban were largely battle-hardened Pashtu. Mullah Muhammad Omar lost his right eye in 1989 when a rocket exploded nearby; Mullah Hassan lost a leg in the war; Justice Minister Nuruddin Turabi and former Foreign Minister Muhammad Ghaus are also one-eyed; the Taliban Mayor of Kabul, Abdul Majid, is missing one leg and two fingers; and other leaders suffer similar disabilities. The wounds were a constant reminder of the 20 years of warfare that devastated Afghanistan. After much discussion, they agreed upon an agenda: restore peace, disarm the population, defend the integrity and Islamic character of Afghanistan, and enforce Sharia (Islamic) law.

Unfortunately, many of the objectives and cultural underpinnings of the Taliban were misunderstood, particularly in the United States. Afghanistan is often said to possess a "warrior society." Its people have long fought to resist external control, but they also have a long tradition of fighting among themselves. While the Taliban were relatively successful in restoring order, they did not hesitate to resort to violence to achieve their objectives. What is often absent in the analysis of such violence is an understanding of the depth of anti-Communist sentiment among the Taliban. Also, it is important to recognize the chaotic and violent nature of Afghan society following the war with the Soviets and the limited control exercised by the mullahs over those who share their beliefs.

Similarly, punishment for crimes such as murder or adultery was often severe and public under the Taliban (although no more so than in many other countries governed by the Sharia). It might also be noted that the Taliban's strict interpretation of Islamic law often resulted in punishments that might be viewed as excessively lenient in non-Islamic countries. For example, in the case of murder, Taliban judges encouraged the families of the victim to accept the payment of *diya*, or blood money, rather than put the killer to death. The purpose was to reduce or eliminate the practice of blood feuds that would result in further violence. As Islamic law was already embedded in Afghan culture, its strict enforcement met with a sharp reduction in crime and widespread public approval.

The treatment of women espoused by the Taliban was also widely criticized, particularly the requirement that women wear the chadri when in public. As in other regions of the Islamic world, Muslim women often view the requirement quite differently from women in non-Islamic societies. For example, as Americans Nancy and Louis Dupree observed:

Women in the cities [of Afghanistan] continue to come out of purdah (*pardah*) and remove the veil, but a strange reversal of attitudes has occurred in villages becoming towns, brought about by the massive shifts of the transport and communication networks in the 1960s. Village and nomadic women seldom wore the *chadri* in the past because it would have interfered with their many daily economic functions. Now, however, if a village grows to town status, complete with a bazaar, and a man gains enough wealth to hire servants, his wife

The Taliban ruled that women must wear the chadri in public, as is being done by these women as they pass the Jame Grand Mosque in Herat.

often insists on wearing a *chadri*, for she believes the custom to be sophisticated and citified—not realizing her city cousins have opposite attitudes. In addition, many young girls in the cities and towns wear the *chadri* briefly after puberty to indicate they have become bona fide women, ready for marriage. (Dupree, 1973)

Further, as noted by Sonia Shah in *The Progressive* (a journal that advocates peace and human rights):

> ... messy reality sometimes confounds [the] captivating idea that the veil victimizes all the women who wear it. A remarkable but underreported Physicians for Human Rights 2000 survey of 200,000 women and men in Afghanistan, for instance, found that more than three-quarters of women in Afghanistan choose to wear the *chadri* with or without the Taliban's edicts, and 90 percent of respondents thought that the Taliban's clothing edicts were an unimportant issue.

Like issues of criminal justice, conflicting views of the role of the chadri in Afghan society were related less to Taliban edicts than to the differing values of rural and urban Afghanistan and the traditional (or folk) and popular (or Westernized) cultures associated with them. In Afghanistan, the former vastly outnumber the latter. But Westernized Afghans, including the Revolutionary Association of the Women of Afghanistan, enjoyed greater access to the Western media and were strongly supported by American groups concerned by reports of wanton violence and the oppression of women. In fact, for many Westernized Afghan women, the Taliban edicts dramatically altered their lives. The following edict relating to women, in its original translation from Dari, was issued after the capture of Kabul in 1996:

> Women you should not step outside your residence. If you go outside the house you should not be like women who used to go with fashionable clothes wearing much cosmetics and appearing in front of every man before the coming of Islam.
>
> Islam ... as a religion has determined specific dignity for Women. Islam has valuable instructions for women. Women should not create such opportunity to attract

the attention of useless people who will not look at them with a good eye. Women have the responsibility as a teacher or coordinator for her family. Husband, brother, father have the responsibility for providing the family with the necessary life requirements (food, clothes, etc.). In case women are required to go outside the residence for the purposes of education, social needs or social services they should cover themselves in accordance with Islamic Sharia regulation. If women are going outside with fashionable, ornamental, tight and charming clothes to show themselves, they will be cursed by the Islamic Sharia and should never expect to go to heaven.

All family elders and every Muslim have responsibility in this respect. We request all family elders to keep tight control over their families and avoid these social problems. Otherwise these women will be threatened, investigated and severely punished as well as the family elders by the forces of the Religious Police (*Munkrat*).

The Religious Police (*Munkrat*) have the responsibility and duty to struggle against these social problems and will continue their effort until evil is finished. (Rashid, 2000)

There were many other edicts: idolatry (worship of objects, rather than God), sorcery, gambling, and the use of addictive substances are unacceptable; female patients should be treated by female physicians; male tailors cannot take measurements of female customers; men should wear beards, but avoid wearing their hair long (in "British and American hairstyles"); music should not be broadcast in public places; music and dancing are to be avoided at weddings; one should avoid playing drums; keeping birds as a hobby must cease; kite flying should be prevented; interest should not be paid for loans; husbands were to be punished should their wives wash clothes in the channels along city streets; and prayer should be performed as required.

This world's tallest statue of Buddah in Bamian, Afghanistan, was 175 feet (53 meters) tall. Taliban soldiers destroyed the head and legs of the statue in March 2001. In April 2002 interim Prime Minister Hamid Karzai vowed to rebuild the two ancient statues, but the source for funds to do this was unclear.

The Taliban strongly opposed efforts in modernization that eroded the cultural integrity of Afghanistan. Many of the efforts toward modernization were associated with atheistic communism. They similarly resented the erosion of moral values as reflected in Hollywood and Indian films, as well as in television serials. The Taliban felt that the films and serials both degraded women and promoted violence. As Donald Wilber observed 40 years ago,

> Westernized Afghans . . . are impatient because they believe that Afghanistan must make extremely rapid economic progress if it is to draw abreast of the modern world, and that the ultimate responsibility for such progress falls upon them. The mass of the people like to keep the good old ways, with a profitable change now and then, and here and there, which does not upset the basic structure. Some, among the more influential of the clergy, would even like to go back to the earlier and 'purer' ways.

The same could be said today.

In many ways, Islamic fundamentalists such as the Taliban are similar to the European Protestants of the 16th century. Like the Protestants, Islamic fundamentalists are a relatively new and innovative presence. As noted by Samuel P. Huntington, both modern Islamic fundamentalism and European Protestantism are reactions to the stagnation and corruption of existing institutions. Both advocate a return to a purer and more demanding form of their religion, and both preach work, order, and discipline. In *The Progressive,* Barbara Ehrenreich describes other similarities:

> In sixteenth-century Swiss cantons and seventeenth-century Massachusetts, Calvinists and Calvinist-leaning Protestants banned dancing, gambling, drinking, colorful clothing, and sports of all kinds. They outlawed idleness and vigorously suppressed sexual activity in all but its married, reproductively oriented, form.
>
> Should he have been transported back into a Calvinist-run Zurich or Salem, a member of the

Taliban or a Wahhabist might have found only one thing that was objectionable: the presence of unveiled women. But he would have been reassured on this point by the Calvinists' insistence on women's subjugation. As a man is to Jesus, asserted the new Christian doctrine, so is his wife to him.

As noted above, throughout history Afghans have resisted rapid social change—particularly imposed change that is both socially disorienting and adversely affects the traditional Afghan way of life, including the means of livelihood. Further, while the Afghan fundamentalists are perhaps a "new and innovative presence," they are oriented by the past, rather than by future expectations. Almost any "modern" action is justified on the basis of history. When an Afghan starts to analyze or explain a problem he will begin by considering its historical aspects.

With regard to governance, many Muslims prefer a theocratic state, such as the Sharia offers. It provides strict standards by which a leader can be judged. Should a leader prove to be unjust, citizens have a right to install new leadership. The attitudes of many Afghans and other Middle Easterners are strongly influenced by a regional history of colonialism, imposed leadership, unresponsive monarchies, and secular dictatorships. Further, Islam provides a coherent alternative framework for the integration of social, economic, and political activity.

Ultimately, the Taliban efforts at social and political reform failed. The fall of the Taliban was variously a consequence of American political and economic interests, gender issues, al-Qaeda's presence in Afghanistan, and an unwillingness to compromise.

Petroleum Politics

With the collapse of the Soviet Union in 1991, the vast gas and oil reserves of Central Asia acquired considerable strategic importance for the United States, as well as for American energy companies. Further, as Ahmed Rashid observed, "US oil companies, who had spearheaded the first US forays into the region, now wanted a greater say in US policy-making." American interests realized that control of Central Asian energy resources would reduce American reliance upon the resources of the Organization of Petroleum Exporting Countries (OPEC). Such control would help avoid petroleum embargoes such as those of the 1970s that posed a threat to industrialized economies. As Sheila Heslin of the National Security Council noted, it was "U.S. policy to promote the rapid development of Caspian energy . . . specifically to promote. . . . Western energy security through diversification of supply."

The area surrounding the Caspian Sea basin ranks among the world leaders in petroleum reserves. But the crude oil, once tapped, must be transported in some way to secure refining and storage facilities before going to commercial markets. The least expensive and safest way to transport the crude oil is by pipeline. Many pipeline routes have been proposed, and these routes, themselves, have become a major political issue. As Russian President Boris Yeltsin commented, "We cannot help seeing the uproar stirred up in some Western countries over the energy resources of the Caspian. Some seek to exclude Russia from the game and undermine its interests. The so-called pipeline war in the region is part of this game."

For a number of reasons, both strategic and economic, the proposed Afghanistan routes were favored by American policy-makers and energy companies. Chronic political instability in countries through which other routes would pass on their way to the Mediterranean Sea posed problems. Further, the American intelligence community had concluded that with German reunification the European Union had become a major competitor. Americans reasoned that it would not be in their long-term national interest for Central Asian gas and oil to pass through the (European controlled) Mediterranean en route to the United States.

The western, or Mediterranean, routes were also longer and correspondingly more difficult to control. The most direct Turkmenistan-Mediterranean route was 1,875 miles (3,017 kilometers) in length; but the most direct route from Turkmenistan to the Arabian Sea, passing through Afghanistan, was only 750 miles (1,207 kilometers) in length. Finally, American energy companies were also intent upon developing Afghanistan pipelines to serve the growing needs of southern and eastern Asia.

In their efforts to establish a trans-Afghanistan pipeline, American energy companies found themselves in competition with Bridas, an Argentinean energy company. Bridas had initiated a feasibility study of an Afghanistan pipeline in March 1995. The following month, the United States set up a working group that included many government agencies and energy companies. Its task was to coordinate American efforts in the exploitation of Central Asia's gas and oil reserves.

When the Taliban gained control of Kabul in September 1996, American governmental officials and the petroleum industry strongly supported them. It was believed that the Taliban were capable of stabilizing the country and establishing a government that could be recognized by the United States. Negotiations regarding the proposed pipeline resulted in Taliban delegations visiting the United States, as well as visits by American officials to Kabul and Kandahar. One American company, Unocal, seeking favor for its desire to develop the region's oil resources, donated $900,000 to the Center of Afghanistan studies at the University of Nebraska at Omaha. The center, in turn, established a training and humanitarian aid program for Afghans. It opened a school at Kandahar to train teachers, electricians, carpenters, and pipe fitters who could assist with the construction of the proposed pipeline. Along with various gifts given to the Taliban and other expenses, the company estimated that it spent $15 to $20 million on the project.

The Argentine company Bridas also courted the Taliban during this period, and their approach was quite different from that of Unocal. The Argentine company executives expressed interest in Islam, as well as the politics, culture, and history of Afghanistan and the Afghans. They also took the trouble to learn the ethnic, tribal, and family linkages of the leaders with whom they met. By contrast, the American company gathered information from the American Embassy in Islamabad and from Pakistani and Turkmen intelligence agencies. It attempted to achieve its objectives through the application of political and economic pressure. Further, its representatives had little apparent knowledge of, or interest in, Afghanistan. "While Bridas engineers would spend hours sipping tea with Afghan tribesmen in the desert as they explored routes," representatives of the American company would "fly in and out and take for granted what they were told by the notoriously fickle Afghan warlords . . . " (Rashid, 2000) The American firm was also at a disadvantage because its policy toward the Taliban did not deviate from the U.S. position; its representatives regularly told the Taliban what they should be doing.

Bridas was ready to sign a deal with the Taliban, even through they were not recognized as the legitimate government by any state. The Taliban did, however, enjoy limited diplomatic recognition, chiefly by conservative states in the Persian Gulf. Taliban support gravitated toward Bridas. In December 1998, the American firm withdrew from the Afghanistan pipeline project consortium, citing low oil prices, concerns about Osama bin Laden being in Afghanistan, and pressure from U.S. feminist groups. The Taliban leaders were quite aware of the potential political and economic costs of their decision.

The Taliban

In the United States, the Taliban lost political support of both Republicans and Democrats, thus greatly increasing their

It is believed that Osama bin Laden may be hiding in Afghanistan, sheltered by the Taliban.

political isolation and vulnerability. Further, both American political parties were able to support a military offensive that would further American strategic objectives. The presence of Osama bin Laden and al-Qaeda in Afghanistan provided policymakers with further justification for a military offensive. Plans for such an offensive began to unfold in 1999 and intensified during the early months of 2001.

Contemporary Muslim political philosophers see existing political boundaries in Southwest Asia as being relics of the colonial past. Today many of them speak out boldly against the values and institutions introduced by the West. Increasingly, they pose a serious threat to many Middle Eastern governments, Westernized Middle Easterners, and Western governments (including those dependent upon the energy resources of the Middle East). While their objectives and approaches vary, many, including Osama bin Laden, direct their energies toward regional unification. They seek to restore a vast region in which the community of Muslims would be united under a single flag. Their vision is bolstered by what many view as the Golden Age of Islam. During this period, extending from the seventh to ninth centuries, Muslim Arab caliphates extended from the Atlantic Ocean into the heart of Central Asia. Some believe that this transformation should be done on a country-by-country basis. Ayatollah Khomeini, for example, transformed Iran from an essentially secular monarchy into an Islamic republic in 1979. Today, many others are searching for mechanisms by which a politically fragmented Middle East can be more quickly transformed into a single Muslim state.

The leaders of this general movement tend to be well educated, affluent, distinguished in battle, and relatively patient. Their most immediate concern is the conflict between Israel and the Palestinians. Other important issues to them are the removal of American troops from Saudi Arabia, and the sanctions imposed upon Iraq. Each of these concerns poses a challenge to American influence in the Middle East. While the Palestinian issue is complicated, most Middle Easterners, regardless of religion, view the creation of Israel as a European solution to a European problem at their expense and without consultation or consent. In their view, Israel continues to reside in the region as an antagonistic European enclave fully supported by the United States.

The Iraqi invasion of Kuwait was widely condemned in the

Middle East. Bin Laden sought to form a Muslim defense force, including battle-hardened "Arab Afghans," to protect Saudi Arabia. Instead, over the objections of Saudi Arabia's senior religious leaders and some members of the royal family, King Fahd permitted American forces to use Saudi Arabia as a base. The United States promised that U.S. troops would not stay in the country "a minute longer than they were needed." More than a decade later, however, some 20,000 American troops remain based in "the country of the Two Holy Places [Mecca and Medina]." While the Iraqi invasion of Kuwait was condemned, even Iraq's staunchest opponents in the region, Iran and Kuwait, object to the United Nations sanctions that followed the conflict.

Ominous clouds of dissent hung over Southwest Asia well before the 2001 American military action against Afghanistan that was triggered by the tragic events of September 11th. In the late spring of 2002, armed conflict continued in Afghanistan, even though the Taliban government and its leadership had been eliminated. Their removal has opened yet another new and uncertain chapter of Afghan history. Achieving lasting stability and peace in Afghanistan remains an elusive and perhaps distant goal.

Sharbat Gula was known as the "Afghan Girl" after she was photographed by Steve McCurry and appeared on the cover of *National Geographic* magazine in 1985. The April 2002 issue documented the photographer's successful search to find her.

6

People
and Culture

The June 1985 edition of *National Geographic* had a photograph on the cover of a young Afghan woman. Her haunting expression and troubled sea-green eyes told of a life of great hardship. The woman came to be known as the "Afghan girl," and her face became one of the world's best-known images. Yet for 17 years, her name, location, and state of well being were unknown to the world. She had first been photographed in a camp for Afghan refugees located in Pakistan.

Seventeen years later, she appeared again on the cover of the April 2002 *National Geographic*. The original photographer, Steve McCurry, had located her in a remote mountain village near Tora Bora. Now perhaps 28 years old (she does not know her age), her face is aged and weathered. Of their meeting, McCurry said, "She's had a hard life. . . . So many here share her story." The mystery woman—now identified as Sharbat Gula—has survived nearly a quarter century of war. During this period of turmoil, an estimated 1.5 million lives have been lost, millions have been injured, and between three and four million Afghans have become refugees. Much of her country lies in ruin. These are just some of the realities that have hardened, and saddened, Sharbat Gula and nearly all other 27 million Afghan people.

Population

Afghanistan's population can only be estimated. Millions of people have died as a result of military activity, hunger, or disease. Millions of others have left the country as refugees to neighboring Pakistan or Iran, or elsewhere. Political instability, poverty, and isolated rural populations scattered about the country's rugged landscape make it all but impossible to take a formal census. It is believed that perhaps 26 to 27 million people live in the country, with another four to five million Afghans living as refugees in neighboring countries. Even though much of the country is mountainous or desert land, its population density is estimated to be 106 people per square mile. In many countries, population density figures are misleading. Whereas the figure is for the country as a whole, huge numbers of people often live in just a few urban centers, leaving much of the rest of the country nearly empty. In Afghanistan, however, only about 20 percent of the people live in cities, leaving nearly 8 out of every 10 scattered about the countryside.

As might be expected in a land ravaged by war, drought, and famine, life expectancy is 45 years—among the shortest in the world. In most countries, women outlive men by a number of years. In Afghanistan, men outlive women by an average of two years. This is one of the few countries in the world where this condition exists. Afghanistan's maternal

Afghan refugees live in neighboring countries. This group is headed to camp in Niatak, Iran.

death rates (death during childbirth) may be the world's highest. The same is true of the country's infant mortality rate; 15 percent of all infants die before reaching one year of age. These tragic conditions are the result of inadequate medical care, lack of sanitary facilities (including clean water), chronic hunger, and the harsh life so many women are forced to endure.

Despite the many problems faced by Afghanistan's people, the population continues to grow at a rate of about 2.4 percent per year. This growth is well above the world average of 1.3 percent gain per year. In fact, it is estimated that the country's population will nearly double—to an estimated 46 million—by 2025. But in a troubled land such as today's Afghanistan, such figures are merely speculation. Many elements—including continued conflict, prolonged drought, accelerated rural-to-urban migration, or further integration of women into society through education and employment—can drastically alter rates of population change. The same elements also can influence migration patterns in or out of the country.

An Ethnically Divided Land

Afghanistan is a country with considerable ethnic diversity. Yet few of the ethnic groups live exclusively in Afghanistan. This reality can seriously erode the country's sense of national identity and integrity. For example, Afghanistan's largest ethnic group, the Pashtun, also reside in neighboring Pakistan, and many are more loyal to their "Pashtunistan" ethnic identity than they are to Afghanistan. Tajiks, Uzbeks, Turkmen, and Kyrgyz also reside in adjacent republics that carry their names (the word *stan*, associated with so many countries in the region simply means "place of"; *Afghanistan*, for example, means "place of the Afghans"). Much of western Afghanistan is simply a cultural extension of Iran. And the related Baluch reside in the drylands of southern Afghanistan, and also in western Pakistan and southeastern Iran. The Brahui generally inhabit the same areas as the Baluch, widely separated from their relatives in southern India. Other groups include the Nuristani, Kohistani, and Gujar who occupy the rugged mountains of eastern Afghanistan and neighboring countries.

ETHNIC GROUPS

This map shows the diverse ethnic makeup of Afghanistan and the areas in which the groups reside.

The country's largest single group, the Pashtun, numbers only about 38 percent of the population. Others with significant numbers include Tajik, 25 percent; Hazara 19, percent; and Uzbek, 6 percent. The small numbers of other minorities amount to a total of about 10 percent of the population. They include Aimaks, Arabs, Baluch, Brahui, Farsiwan, Gujar, Hindus, Jat Guji (traders claiming Arab descent), Jews, Kohistani, Kyrgyz, Mughal, Nuristani, Pamiri, Qizilbash, Sikhs, Turkmen, and a few others. Many of the ethnic groups, particularly the Pashtu, are further divided into various tribal units. The principal tribal divisions of the Pashtu are the Durrani, found chiefly in southern Afghanistan, and the Ghilzai of eastern Afghanistan. Sharp divisions along ethnic and tribal lines are one of the greatest problems Afghanistan faces. It is difficult to politically unify such a culturally diverse people.

Language

Language is perhaps the single most important element that binds people together as ethnic groups. A society that is able to communicate among its members is more apt to share common ideas, values, information, views, and other traits. As is amply illustrated by so many conflicts ongoing in the world today, a society divided by language can be difficult to unify. Language differences pose yet another problem for Afghanistan as it works toward integrating all its diverse population into a socially unified state. Four major language families are represented in Afghanistan: Indo-European, Altaic, Dravidian, and Afro-Asiatic (Semitic). A language family is a major language group that, through time, may have branched into many different, yet distantly related, languages. Most languages spanning an area extending from Western Europe to Hindi-speaking India, for example, fall into the Indo-European family.

Afghanistan's two most widely spoken languages, Pashtu

and Dari (Afghan Farsi or Persian), are Indo-European. Both serve as "official" languages. Dari, the language most commonly used in commerce and the media, serves as a lingua franca (a language spoken in common by people who otherwise speak their own language). It is generally believed that the Brahui speakers are the oldest resident population in Afghanistan. They were also the principal ethnic component of the Indus Civilization (Indus Valley of present-day Pakistan). Indo-European-speakers first arrived some 4,000 years ago. They conquered the Brahui and established major kingdoms, including Bactria and Arachosia. The Altaic- and Semitic-speakers are more recent arrivals.

Religion

Formal religious systems have varied considerably through time in Afghanistan. In the past, the area was heavily influenced by shamanistic traditions, many of which still influence Afghan society. Shamanism is a folk religious tradition that is carried out under the leadership of a shaman. This is particularly true of isolated societies in the Hindu Kush mountainous region. This area of Central Asia gave birth to several religious traditions. Among them, Afghanistan was the original home of Zoroastrianism. This faith—with its dualistic traditions, such as good and evil and angels and devils—significantly influenced Judaism, Greek thought, and Christianity, as well as religious systems elsewhere in Asia. Zoroastrianism served as the state religion during the seventh-century Sassanian period.

Hinduism may have reached Afghanistan over the trade routes from the east some time during the third century B.C.E. Today, some 20,000 Hindus live in Afghanistan. Buddhism also became an important religion in Afghanistan. It was introduced during the first century A.D. There is reason to believe that Judaism entered Afghanistan early in the first millennium, and there is still a Jewish presence in the country. Most members of this faith live in Kabul, Kandahar, and Herat, where they work as merchants, traders, and moneylenders. By the fifth century, Nestorian Christianity had entered Afghanistan. It soon became the accepted Christian denomination of the Persian Empire. Islam entered Central Asia in the mid-seventh century and rapidly became the dominant religion in Afghanistan and throughout the rest of the region. Today, about 85 percent of the Afghan Muslims follow Sunni Islam, while 15 percent are adherents of Shiite sects. Finally, there has long been a resident Sikh population—a group centered in northern India. They are the most recent religious arrival, and most Sikhs are engaged in commerce.

Living in Afghanistan Today

With so many social, ethnic, and cultural aspects of Afghanistan in disarray, the nuclear family once again is the most important social unit. Afghan families are very tightly knit. Extended families or clans are also extremely important. During periods of social upheaval, even ethnic affiliation becomes increasingly important to people. In other words, when people are under extreme stress, they look inward. They seek comfort and protection—and an essential sense of "belonging"—within the smallest social units with which they identify.

Over the decades that have lapsed since the Soviet military offensive in the late 1970s, life has been extremely difficult for the Afghans. The human toll as measured by loss of life and limb has been staggering. Families have been fragmented and interpersonal and interethnic relations have been seriously eroded. The American-led military action that began late in 2001 has further disrupted Afghan society. As was true during the decade of Soviet involvement in the country, it is accompanied by the introduction of social and economic values incompatible with those of many Afghans.

Life in Afghanistan today is extremely difficult. Families have had to develop coping strategies to survive. Some send sons into combat; others send family members to other countries to find work and to be able to send money to the family left behind. Above all, they hope to protect their children from harm and simply make ends meet in terms of day-to-day survival. No country in the world has more households headed by women, or men crippled by warfare, than does Afghanistan. This circumstance increases the vulnerability of families in an increasingly disoriented society. Some relief has been felt by Westernized, urban Afghans able to again enjoy Western entertainment, other forms of recreation, and less restrictive interpersonal relations. For the vast majority of Afghans, however—those who adhere to more traditional values—the present is challenging and the future is uncertain.

Interim leader Hamid Karzai speaks at a news conference in February 2002.
He answered questions about the killing of civil aviation and tourism minister
Abdul Rahman.

Government and Economy

I n Afghanistan, as is true of many other countries throughout the world, government and economy are closely linked. A strong, stable government creates an environment in which an economy can thrive and a country's people can prosper. When government is weak and a country is constantly in turmoil, its economy almost certainly will fail. Not surprisingly, considering its recent history, Afghans today rank among the world's poorest people.

Government

During the 20th century, the design of Afghanistan's official flag has changed nearly 20 times. By the time this book is published, it may be changed again. Conflict among different groups over the most appropriate symbol to represent the country—the design of its flag—is just one example that illustrates the political instability that has plagued the country throughout most of its history. Afghanistan has experienced a dizzying flow of different governments over the years.

It is believed that the tribal societies of ancient Afghanistan were governed much as they are today. Leadership was provided by headmen, councils of elders, and perhaps shamans, or religious leaders. Throughout Afghan history, multiple systems of governance have coexisted.

Spatially, as is true in the United States, some political decisions have been and continue to be made at a local level. In Afghanistan, such decisions were usually tribal in nature. Above this level, there was generally a hierarchy in which one or more systems were dominant. In part, the plural nature of governance reflected Afghanistan's distance from centers of power. For example, the highest level of authority during much of the country's early history was in the hands of powerful, distant powers. Because they were remote, their power often was limited and considerable freedom was permitted with regard to local government.

During the early years of Islamic expansion, Afghanistan was still somewhat remote from the centers of power. The situation soon changed, however. Different levels of governance do continue to exist in the predominantly Islamic society of Afghanistan. But Islam is much more prescriptive than most other religious systems—the religion, itself, strongly influences how people are governed. Therefore, not only religious beliefs, but also social and economic activity are strongly influenced by Islam. And the way people are governed under Islamic laws tend to be much more uniform than in the past. This is the case despite the presence of varying Islamic sects and schools of law.

Recent years have witnessed a struggle between secular (not tied to religion) and religious governance. The formation of an independent Afghan government began when Great Britain relinquished control over Afghanistan's foreign affairs.

That date, August 19, 1919, is still recognized as the country's independence day. In 1926, King Amanullah visited Europe and countries of the eastern Mediterranean. He was greatly impressed by what he saw and attempted to apply his vision of modernization to Afghanistan. His efforts, however, were strongly rejected by a council of traditional leaders, the *Loya Jirgeh*. Since that time—more than three-quarters of a century ago—there has been an almost constant struggle between religious beliefs, government, and society. Some people and governments want to liberalize society and make government more secular. On the other hand, there are many people who resist change. They prefer to adhere to a traditional way of life and want to maintain systems of society and governance directed by Islamic laws.

The traditional approach was that taken by the Taliban. When they came to power in the mid-1990s, they referred to Afghanistan as the "Islamic Emirate of Afghanistan." This tie between country and religious faith was an echo of the powerful emirates of the country's Islamic past. It was also the foundation for what they hoped would become a modern caliphate—a state under Islamic rule. The transitional government established following the fall of the Taliban in 2002 appears to have little popular authority. As this book goes to press, the constitution remains suspended and the central government has not gained control. Separate ethnic factions effectively govern the various parts of country. In the recent past, all factions had agreed to follow Sharia, or Islamic law. Afghanistan's many political parties essentially reflect ethnic units and relationships. The 30 provinces of Afghanistan continue to provide a more formal framework for political activity. Afghanistan also belongs to several regional and international organizations. Today, agencies of the United Nations are playing particularly important roles in their attempt to bring stability to the country and to help its people survive these trying times.

Economy

Afghanistan's earliest economy was based on hunting and gathering. It was the ancient people of this region, however, who were among the first to domesticate plants and engage in cultivation. In addition to the rain-fed cultivation of cereals, such as barley and wheat, southeastern Afghanistan was closely linked to one of the world's earliest irrigation civilizations—the high culture that arose on the fertile flood plains of the Indus River Valley. It was also an area prominent in animal domestication. Village-based livestock systems were joined by systems of pastoral nomadism when Aryans arrived in the region as early as the second millennium B.C.E. Traditional systems of cultivation and pastoral nomadism continue to be very important to Afghanistan's economy and millions of its rural people. Today, however, the traditional systems of farming increasingly compete with modern irrigation projects in both northern and southern Afghanistan. And the number of people and herds following the wandering way of life of the pastoral nomad is in sharp decline.

Much of Afghanistan receives scant precipitation and has rugged terrain. Considering its physical geography, it is little wonder that only some 12 percent of the country is suited to farming. Barley and wheat remain the principal cereals. They are now joined by corn (maize), millet, rice, and rye. Many types of fruit are grown in Afghanistan, including apples, apricots, and cherries, as well as dates, figs, and grapes. Afghan grapes are exported to markets throughout southern Asia. In warmer southern parts of the country, even bananas are grown. Several varieties of nuts also thrive, including almonds, pistachios, and walnuts. Garden crops are important to a people who do not have the luxury of purchasing their food from a supermarket. Asparagus, beans, beets, brussels sprouts, and cabbage are found in nearly every home garden; so are carrots, cucumbers, mustard, onions, potatoes, and pumpkins.

This shopkeeper sells cloth from inside a large metal shipping container that was left behind by its owners during a time of conflict in Afghanistan.

Still other important crops include varieties of hay, particularly alfalfa and clover, used in feeding livestock, cotton, sugarcane, and tobacco. One important crop that has international implications is the opium poppy—the source of a powerful narcotic. The Taliban banned the planting of opium poppies. Since the removal of the Taliban by U.S. forces, opium has again become an important crop.

Livestock include cattle, sheep, goats, donkeys, horses, and camels. Fowl such as chickens, ducks, and geese are also kept. Afghanistan is famous for its high-grade karakul (a variety of sheep) pelts. Wool and mutton are also important exports.

Afghanistan has a variety of mineral resources. Its energy resources include coal, natural gas, and some petroleum. The country also has reserves of copper, iron ore, lead, and zinc.

Unfortunately, its energy and metals have given rise to only minimal industrial development. Afghanistan also has a great variety of precious and semiprecious gemstones. Many people believe that Afghanistan possesses a vast amount of undeveloped—and perhaps as yet undiscovered—mineral wealth.

Most of Afghanistan's industrial products are based upon the country's agricultural and natural resources. From its livestock come carpets, foods, shoes, soap, and textiles. Processed foods come from both livestock and crops. Furniture is made from wood gained from the country's forests and may also use leather, from animal skins. Coal, natural gas, and petroleum are used as energy and also in the manufacture of some products. Copper is worked into various useful items, including containers. Hamid Karzai, who in 2001 began serving as transitional president, was previously employed by the Unocal petroleum company. It is therefore probable that Afghanistan will attach particular importance to its role in the further development of Central Asia's energy resources.

During recent years, trade between Afghanistan and other countries has suffered. In addition to the disruption caused directly by warfare, the country has lost much of its ability to produce, purchase, or distribute commodities of any kind. Traditionally, its major trading partners are the countries of the former Soviet Union, Pakistan, and Iran, with lesser amounts of trade with several other Asian countries. Trade with Western industrial countries is quite limited.

Afghanistan has a potential labor force of about seven million, nearly 70 percent of whom are engaged in agriculture. Only about 10 percent of the people are employed in industry—a figure that ranks very low among the world's nations. A scant 10 percent of the population is involved in construction or commerce. If the war-torn country stabilizes and international aid is received to rebuild, the construction sector of the economy is sure to experience huge future growth.

Finally, about 10 percent of the population is engaged in services and other occupations.

Decades of violence and years of drought have combined to severely reduce agricultural productivity. In 2002 many Afghan people face hunger, and some regions are experiencing famine. The growing of drug-producing opium poppies—outlawed by the now deposed Taliban—is once again becoming widespread. The illegal narcotics derived from the plant have high value in the world market. With government restrictions now removed, many farmers grow poppies to compensate for the loss of other crops to drought, danger imposed by the enormous number of land mines in rural areas, and continuing armed conflict. The country's gross domestic product has dropped to a low $21 billion. Roughly 50 percent of its wealth is derived from agricultural production. Another 30 percent comes from industry, and about 20 percent is gained from a variety of services. Per capita income is approximately $800 a year. The country's economy continues to struggle and remains one of the world's poorest. This is a very sad state for a country that offers so much potential, both in terms of its natural and human resources.

Women are no longer forced to keep their faces completely covered as they were under the Taliban and are allowed more freedom to visit public places now that the conservative Taliban government has been replaced.

8

Afghanistan Looks Ahead

T he history of Afghanistan suggests that the country will continue to experience a tug-of-war in terms of values. Some people will seek to make the country more modern—to undergo a cultural leap of perhaps a century or more. Others, those who fear modern ways and their accompanying loss of traditional values and other ways of life, will continue to resist change. A major conflict of the 20th century—that of tradition versus modernization and its accompanying changes—is certain to be a major issue well into the 21st century.

Afghanistan was never effectively colonized. Therefore, the country does not need to pass through a painful period of decolonization (the process of learning how to function as an independent country). In terms of the future, perhaps neighboring Iran can be looked to as a possible "model." That country experienced several major cultural and political revolutions during the last half of the 20th century. Until 1979, a shah who attempted to modernize the country governed Iran. His often harsh rule and rapid steps toward modernization caused much dissention. Ultimately, he was forced into exile and was replaced by a religious fundamentalist who declared the country to be an Islamic republic subject to Islamic laws. By 1999, however, there were signs that the government of Iran was relaxing many of its rules and beginning to look outward toward the global community. As has happened in Iran, Afghanistan can return to many of its traditional cultural roots; its society can evolve into one that is stabilized by shared core values; it can address environmental and social issues of importance; and it can be open to collaboration with the West. Although Afghans resisted colonial encroachment, and greatly resent the armed intrusions of the Soviets and Americans, they do appreciate Western technology and have historically maintained close ties with the West.

The future of Afghanistan, as well as other Muslim countries, depends heavily upon a better informed and more understanding and tolerant West. It is particularly important that the United States, as the world's only remaining superpower, reconsider its role on the global stage. The "rights" and "wrongs" of U.S. military involvement in Afghanistan will be debated for decades. Certainly, Americans were outraged by the events of September 11, 2001. Few people would argue whether Osama bin Laden acted as a ruthless terrorist. But in the process of seeking and punishing this one individual with his small group of supporters much of a country was laid to waste.

Afghans and other Middle Easterners "think historically." And much of the history that they recall is one of manipulation and humiliation by foreigner aggressors. Perceived insult and other grievances, as well as access to advanced technology, have bred a new and more ominous form of militancy than the world has known in the past. Its destructive impacts have been seen in recent years. The time has come to develop more inclusive systems of international commerce and governance— systems more sensitive to culture and circumstance. It would be in such a new world order that Afghans might find fulfillment and security.

If these goals are to be achieved, many things can and must happen if Afghanistan and its people are to rise from the ashes of recent flaming conflicts. First and foremost, Afghanistan's diverse ethnic groups must work toward achieving a common goal of nationality—a people who share a common sense of "belonging" as a single group. This will be difficult to achieve in a land where tribalism and ethnicity have long been the highest level of group allegiance. The role of women in society must be improved greatly. Women must receive equal protection under the law, and be allowed to pursue their personal goals in terms of education, employment, and childbearing. No society can prosper when a substantial portion of its resources—in this context, human—remain underdeveloped. The country must be rebuilt. Many of its cities, much of its transportation network, large parts if its power and communications facilities, and nearly all of its agricultural and industrial capacity lie in ruin. Rebuilding will take time, billions of dollars, huge amounts of labor, and the further introduction of outside capital, technology, and values.

If Afghanistan is unable to overcome these obstacles, the country's future is bleak. On the other hand, if it able to overcome its many problems—and there are growing signs that this can be accomplished—it has the natural and human resource potential to become a strong and stable country.

Facts at a Glance

Land and People

Official Name	Islamic State of Afghanistan
Location	In Central Asia, bordered by Turkmenistan, Uzbekistan, and Tajikistan to the north; by China to the northeast; by Pakistan to the south and east; and by Iran to the west
Area	653,089 square kilometers (252,092 square miles)
Climate	A dry midlatitude climate in the northern lowlands; undifferentiated highland climates in mountainous regions; a dry tropical climate in the southern lowlands
Capital	Kabul
Other Cities	Herat, Kandahar, Mazar-e Sharif
Population	26,813,057 (July 2001 estimate)
Population Distribution	Rural, 80 percent; urban, 20 percent
Major Rivers	Amu Darya, Hari Rud, Helmand, Kabul
Mountains	Hindu Kush, Selseleh-ye Safed Koh (Paropamisus)
Highest Point	Nowshak, 7,485 meters (24,557 feet)
Official Languages	Pashtu; Dari (Afghan Farsi)
Other Languages	More than 30 languages variously representing the Indo-European, Altaic, Dravidian, and Afro-Asiatic families
Ethnic Groups	Pashtun, 38 percent; Tajik, 25 percent; Hazara, 19 percent; Uzbek, 6 percent; others (including Aimaks, Arabs, Baluch, Brahui, Farsiwan, Gujar, Hindus, Jat Guji, Jews, Kohistani, Kyrgyz, Mughal, Nuristani, Pamiri, Qizilbash, Sikhs, and Turkmen), 12 percent
Religions	Sunni Islam, 84 percent; Shiite Islam, 15 percent; others (including Christians, Hindus, Jews, Sikhs, and Zoroastrians), 1 percent
Literacy Rate	31.5 percent
Average Life Expectancy	Males, 46.97 years; females, 45.47 years

Economy

Natural Resources	Coal, natural gas, petroleum; barites, chromite, copper, iron ore, lead, salt, sulfur, talc, zinc; precious and semiprecious stones
Division of Labor Force	Agriculture, 67.8 percent; industry, 10.2 percent; construction, 6.3 percent; commerce, 5 percent; services and other occupations, 10.7 percent
Agricultural Products	Fruit, nuts, vegetables, wheat; medicinals, opium poppies, spices; karakul pelts, mutton, wool
Industries	Carpet weaving, cement, fertilizer, food processing, furniture, natural gas, mining, petroleum refining, shoes, soap, textiles
Major Imports	Food and petroleum products; most consumer goods
Major Exports	Handwoven carpets, cotton, fruit, precious and semiprecious stones, hides and pelts, nuts, opium poppies, wool
Currency	Afghani

Government

Form of Government	Provisional central government; effective administration by rural, ethnic factions
Governmental Bodies	The formal executive and legislative branches of government have been dissolved; judicial decisions are based upon Islamic law
Formal Head of State	Provisional president
Voting Rights	Currently undetermined

History at a Glance

11,000 B.C.E.	Archaeological evidence indicates the presence of settled agricultural populations in southern Afghanistan.
4th Millennium B.C.E.	South-central regions of Afghanistan are intimately associated with the Indus Civilization; a relationship that persists into the second millennium B.C.E.
6th Century B.C.E.	The kingdoms of Bactria and Sogdiana are established in Afghanistan. The prophet Zoroaster rises to prominence in Bactria. The region is later incorporated into the Archaemenid Empire.
331 B.C.E.	Bactria, Sogdiana, and surrounding regions fall to forces of Alexander III of Macedon (Alexander the Great). Greco-Bactrian dominance continues until ca. 130 B.C.E.
Mid-7th Century	Islam expands into Afghanistan.
10th-12th Centuries	The Ghaznavid Empire, among the most important indigenous Afghan empires, flourishes during this period. It extends from Kurdistan to Kashmir and is known for its patronage of the arts, literature, and science.
13th Century	Invasions by Mongol and Turco-Mongol forces. Particularly destructive are the 1220 and 1221 campaigns of Genghis Khan.
16th Century	From the sixteenth through the seventeenth century, Afghanistan is contested between the Persian Safavids and Indian Mughals.
19th Century	Great Britain and Russia seek control over Afghanistan in what has become known as the Great Game. Anglo-Afghan wars occur in 1839-1842 and 1878-1880.
1893	The Durand Line separating Afghanistan and British India is drawn through the midst of the Pashtun tribal lands, thus serving as a basis for subsequent conflict between Afghanistan and Pakistan.
1936	Afghanistan signs a trade agreement with the Soviet Union and a treaty of friendship with the United States.
1964	A constitution providing for a democratic government is drafted, but lack of agreement on its provisions prevents implementation.
1979	Soviets dispatch 85,000 troops to Afghanistan at the request of Prime Minister Amin. He is then assassinated and replaced by Babrak Karmal—a more moderate leader supported by the Soviets. Mullahs and khans declare a jihad, and mujaheddin guerrillas attack government and Soviet troops.
1988	A peace accord is signed by Afghanistan, Pakistan, the Soviet Union, and the United States.
1994	Conflict increases among ethnic factions; the Taliban captures Kandahar as a first step in their effort to stabilize the country.
1996	The Taliban gain control of Kabul. American support for the Taliban increases.
1999	The United States initiates United Nations economic sanctions punishing the Taliban for providing sanctuary to Osama bin Laden. Discussions regarding an American military offensive against the Taliban government and al-Qaeda continue.
2001	Terrorist attacks in the United States attributed to al-Qaeda trigger a massive military offensive designed to curb terrorism.
2002	A provisional government is established in Kabul; the military offensive continues.

*B.C.E. is Before the Common Era

Further Reading

Bodansky, Yossef. *Bin Laden: The Man Who Declared War on America.* Rocklin, C.A.: Prima Publishing, 1999.

Cohen, Saul B., ed. *The Columbia Gazetteer of the World.* New York: Columbia University Press, 1998. Vol. 1.

Hopkirk, Peter. *The Great Game: On Secret Service in High Asia.* London: John Murray, 1990.

McEvedy. Colin. The *Penguin Atlas of Medieval History.* Harmondsworth, England: Penguin Books, 1961.

Sabini, John. *Islam: A Primer.* Washington, D.C.: Middle East Editorial Associates, 1983.

Textor, Robert B. *Cultural Frontiers of the Peace Corps.* Cambridege, M.A.: MIT Press, 1966.

Arberry, A.J. *The Legacy of Persia.* Oxford at the Clarendon Press, 1953.

Bergen, Peter L. *Holy War, Inc.: Inside the Secret World of Osama bin Laden.* New York: Free Press, 2001.

Central Intelligence Agency. *The World Factbook—Afghanistan.* (*http://www.cia.gov/cia/publications/factbook/index/html*)

Collins, Joseph J. *The Soviet Invasion of Afghanistan: A Study in the Use of Force in Soviet Foreign Policy.* Lexington, M.A.: Lexington Books, 1986.

Department of the Army. *Area Handbook for Afghanistan.* (Pamphlet 550-65, 4th edition.) Washington, D.C., 1973.

Douglas, William O. *Beyond the High Himalaya.* Garden City, N.Y.: Doubleday, 1952.

Dupree, Louis. *Afghanistan.* Princeton, N.J: Princeton University Press, 1973.

Efendi, Evliya. *Narrative of Travels in Europe, Asia, and Africa, in the Seventeenth Century.* (Joseph von Hammer, trans.) London: Oriental Translation Fund of Great Britain and Ireland, 1846.

Ehrenreich, Barbara. "Christian Wahhabists." *The Progressive*, January 2002.

Frye, Richard N. *The Heritage of Persia.* Cleveland, O.H.: World Publishing Company, 1963.

Khrushchev, Nikita. *Khrushchev Remembers.* (Strobe Talbott, trans. and ed.) London: Andre Deutsch, 1971.

Mackinder, H.J. *Democratic Ideas and Reality.* New York: Henry Holt, 1919.

National Geographic Society. *Afghanistan and Pakistan.* Washington, D.C.: National Geographic Society, December 2001.

Nollau, Gunther and Wiche, Hans J. *Russia's South Flank.* New York: Praeger, 1963.

Rashid, Ahmed. *Taliban: Militant Islam, Oil and Fundamentalism in Central Asia.* New Haven: C.T.: Yale University Press, 2000.

Shah, Sonia. "Veiled Solidarity." *The Progressive*, January 2002.

Wilber, Donald N. *Afghanistan: Its People, Its Society, Its Culture.* New Haven, C.T.: HRAF Press, 1962.

Index

Index

page:

8:	© Reuters NewMedia Inc./CORBIS	60:	AP/Wide World Photos
11:	© AFP/CORBIS	62:	AP/Wide World Photos
14:	21st Century Publishing	65:	© Reuters NewMedia Inc./CORBIS
16:	© AFP/CORBIS	70:	AP/Wide World Photos
21:	© Carl & Ann Purcell/CORBIS	73:	AP/Wide World Photos
23:	© Ric Ergenbright/CORBIS	79:	AP/Wide World Photos
24:	21st Century Publishing	82:	© Steve McCurry/Magnum Photos
28:	© Webistan/CORBIS	85:	© AFP/CORBIS
33:	AP/Wide World Photos	87:	Reprinted from Dupree, Louis.

8: © Reuters NewMedia Inc./CORBIS
11: © AFP/CORBIS
14: 21st Century Publishing
16: © AFP/CORBIS
21: © Carl & Ann Purcell/CORBIS
23: © Ric Ergenbright/CORBIS
24: 21st Century Publishing
28: © Webistan/CORBIS
33: AP/Wide World Photos
38: Reprinted from Chardin, John. Travels in
     Persia: 1637-1677. London: J. Smith, 1720
41: © Reuters NewMedia Inc./CORBIS
44: © Hulton-Deutsch Collection/CORBIS
46: AP/Wide World Photos
53: © Reuters NewMedia Inc./CORBIS

60: AP/Wide World Photos
62: AP/Wide World Photos
65: © Reuters NewMedia Inc./CORBIS
70: AP/Wide World Photos
73: AP/Wide World Photos
79: AP/Wide World Photos
82: © Steve McCurry/Magnum Photos
85: © AFP/CORBIS
87: Reprinted from Dupree, Louis.
     Afghanistan. Princeton: Princeton
     Universtiy Press, 1973
92: AP/Wide World Photos
97: AP/Wide World Photos
100: AP/Wide World Photos

Cover: © Baci/CORBIS

Frontis: Flag courtesy of *www.theodora.com/flags*. Used by permision.

About the Author

JEFFREY A. GRITZNER is the chairman of the Department of Geography, the Asian Studies Program, and the International and Cultural Diversity Cluster at the University of Montana. He coordinates the Montana Geographic Alliance and is chairman of the Great Plains/Rocky Mountain Division of the Association of American Geographers.

CHARLES F. "FRITZ" GRITZNER is Distinguished Professor of Geography at South Dakota State University. He is now in his fifth decade of college teaching and research. Much of his career work has focused on geographic education. Fritz has served as both president and executive director of the National Council for Geographic Education and has received the Council's George J. Miller Award for Distinguished Service.